Old World
Stitchery
for Today

1 Warsaw
2 Krakow
3 Pszczyna
4 Dabrowa Tarnowska
5 Tarnow
6 Rzeszow
7 Lancut
8 Lowicz
9 Piotrkow
10 Sieradz
11 Poznan

*12 White Forest Kurpie
*13 Green Forest Kurpie
14 Szczawnica
15 Limanowa
*16 Kaszuby
*17 Zagorzanie
18 Zywiec
19 Makow Podhalanski
*20 Podhale

* indicates ethnographic areas

Polish Eyelet Embroidery, Cutwork,
Goldwork, Beadwork, Drawn Thread
and Other Techniques

OLD WORLD
STITCHERY
FOR TODAY

Grażyna J. Kozaczka

Chilton Book Company

Radnor, Pennsylvania

To my grandmother and my mother,
who built the foundations of my knowledge,
and to my husband,
who always gave me encouragement
and technical assistance

Copyright © 1987 by Grażyna J. Kozaczka
All Rights Reserved
Published in Radnor, Pennsylvania 19089, by Chilton Book Company

All drawings by the author;
all black-and-white and color photos by Stanley J. Kozaczka;
all items, unless otherwise indicated, are from the
private collection of Stanley and Grażyna Kozaczka.
Designed by William E. Lickfield
Manufactured in the United States of America

Library of Congress Cataloging in Publication Data
Kozaczka, Grażyna J., 1955–
Old world stitchery for today.
Bibliography p. 226
Includes index.
1. Embroidery—Poland.   2. Decoration and
ornament—Poland.   I. Title.
TT769.P7K69   1987   746.44'028   87–47731
ISBN 0–8019–7732–0

1 2 3 4 5 6 7 8 9 0   6 5 4 3 2 1 0 9 8 7

Contents

List of stitches continues on next page

Introduction

Few countries in Europe could match Poland in its variety of folk costume. This fact alone underscored the extreme importance Polish peasants attached to their costumes. Costumes, after all, differentiated a certain region, village, or economic group and also signified the function of the costume wearer within the group—even his or her marital status. The costumes were true works of art, where textures and colors were combined in a composition that inspired both admiration and envy. For the peasantry, costumes were the sole luxuries of an otherwise frugal and hardworking people. To achieve this effect of luxury, needleworkers used the highest-quality materials and combined them with many decorative techniques, such as embroidery, beadwork, cutwork, and lacework.

Because these techniques were employed mainly in creating costumes, I felt it was crucial to devote part of the book to describing a variety of costumes, their construction, decoration, and, to some degree, their functions. I also devoted some space to a discussion of the folk artists themselves in order to make their work more understandable to the contemporary needleworker. As with so many other forms of folk art, artists remain mainly anonymous and only general information about their technique and living conditions is available. The evidence of their work—finished and surviving articles of clothing—is easier to find in ethnographic museums or in private collections.

Through historical, sociological, and technical discussions on these various needlework techniques, I hope to make this book an enjoyable one to read, look at, and use. Through it I want to convey my love of needlework and Polish folklore; to acquaint the reader with the wealth of Polish traditional needlework and show its connection with the achievements of other countries; to remind needleworkers of some lesser known or even a few forgotten techniques; and to give needleworkers a chance to work on some practical projects that incorporate traditional Polish folk designs.

1

The practical needlework projects fall into two distinct categories. The first category includes items I designed on the basis of old folk patterns found mainly on traditional costumes. The other category comprises items from my collection that were stitched in Poland by anonymous folk needleworkers and for which I try to provide technical instructions.

1

Basic Stitches
and Technical Notes

MATERIALS

Most of the projects presented here are stitched on fabrics made from natural fibers: cotton, linen, and cotton/linen blends. Only tulle (English net) and some velvets are of man-made fibers. I have always tried to select natural fibers because I wanted to stay as close as possible to the traditional materials used by Polish folk needleworkers. The same is true of the threads used. I try to select cotton embroidery flosses, or pearl cotton, which, unlike six-stranded floss, comes in only one strand, is twisted, and has much more sheen. I had to cut corners on goldwork because of the cost of precious metals, but good results can be achieved with several kinds of metallic threads. For the couching thread, I used shiny, twisted silk because it blends perfectly with metallic yarns.

When choosing materials, be guided by quality and select only the very best. Consider how many hours of work you will devote to completing a project, and don't diminish the final effect of the finished item with poor-quality materials.

TOOLS

I have followed Polish folk traditions regarding needlework tools. Thus, for only a few projects have I used round embroidery hoops, while most items should be held freely in hand. Embroidery hoops, however, are a must if you have problems with thread tension. It is much easier to achieve the right tension when the fabric is stretched on a hoop.

Good sharp embroidery scissors and sharp sewing scissors are absolutely necessary for all the projects. For some of the eyelet designs, you

Fig. 1-1 Six-stranded embroidery floss in a range of colors.

will also need a stiletto, a sharp peg made of wood or plastic that is used for piercing the fabric and making round eyelets.

An optional tool is a thimble. I prefer leather fingerguards, which look like single fingers cut off from a glove, because they offer protection without impairing the feeling in the finger.

While discussing tools, we cannot forget the needles that are so crucial to every needleworker. The size of a needle should be selected according to the thread used and the background fabric on which the design is placed. If the eye of the needle is too small, the thread will fray. If the needle is too thick for the fabric, it will leave holes that will be visible even after the work is completed. For beading, I use special long, slim beading needles.

Other tools useful in working on needlework projects are pins, pencils, carbon paper, tracing paper, masking tape, and an iron for transferring designs.

4

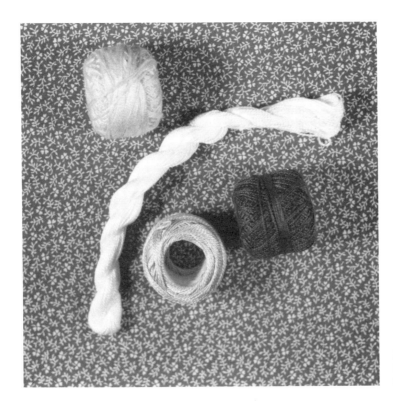

Fig. 1–2 Pearl cotton in balls and skeins.

TRANSFERRING DESIGNS FROM PAPER TO FABRIC

Even before you start the project and trace the design onto the fabric, it is a good idea to hem all the raw edges of the fabric or at least secure them with masking tape to avoid fraying the fabric as you work.

There are several methods of transferring needlework designs from paper to fabric. The method you choose will depend on the background fabric you select and on your drawing skill.

Freehand Transfer

Freehand transfer demands a considerable amount of drawing skill and a good eye. The pattern is drawn on the fabric with a soft lead pencil, following the original design.

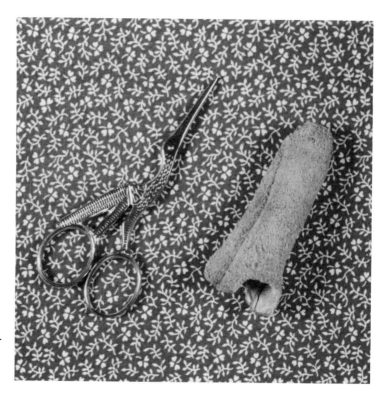

Fig. 1–3 Stork embroidery scissors and a leather fingerguard.

Tracing with Dressmaker's Carbon

Tracing with dressmaker's carbon paper ensures good results if you are less skilled in freehand drawing, especially if you select a smooth background fabric.

Place the fabric on a smooth, hard surface and cover it with a sheet of dressmaker's carbon paper placed with its inked side toward the fabric. Place the design on top of the paper. Pin all three layers—fabric, carbon paper, and the pattern sheet—together in several places to keep them secure while you trace the design. Trace the outlines of the pattern with a pencil or a dry ballpoint pen. Be careful as you draw so that you don't pierce and tear the pattern and the carbon sheet.

Select the carbon paper in a color to match the color of the background fabric. On light-colored fabrics, use only light-colored carbons so the drawing will not show through after you complete the stitching.

6

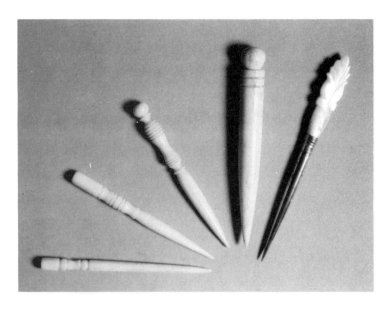

Fig. 1–4 A collection of stilettos for making eyelets.

Tracing on Glass

Another method of transferring the pattern is to trace it on a glass table. This method requires a powerful source of light and a table or a stand with a glass top. First, position the lamp underneath the glass. Then place the pattern on top of the glass and cover it with the background fabric. Tape both layers to the glass to hold them securely. When the lamp is turned on, the design will show clearly on the fabric and can be traced with a soft lead pencil.

Running-Stitch Transfer

Running-stitch transfer is used especially when working with fabrics with a nap, such as velvet. Transfer the pattern to a sheet of soft tracing paper or tissue paper and place it directly on the background fabric. Pin both layers securely together and cover all the lines of the pattern with a running stitch executed through both the paper and background fabric. Always use a thread color that will contrast sharply with the color of the fabric.

After you have covered all the lines with the stitching, tear off the tracing paper piece by piece, so that all that is left on the background fabric is the design "drawn" with the running stitch. Use a soft tracing paper

Fig. 1–5 The first stage in transferring a design to velvet: trace a design with running stitches executed through both paper and velvet.

so that you can remove it easily without damaging the stitching and blurring the pattern.

ENLARGING AND REDUCING DESIGNS

To change the size of an original design, draw a grid of identical squares over the pattern. Then prepare a second grid with the same number of squares as the first one, but make the squares smaller or larger. If you want to enlarge the pattern, make the squares larger than the original ones, and if you are reducing the pattern, make the squares smaller. Then copy the design freehand square by square from the original drawing to the new grid.

Fig. 1–6 After the paper is torn off, the design stays on the velvet, "drawn" in running stitch.

You can also enlarge and reduce patterns on many photocopiers, but some minor distortions in the pattern may result.

STITCHES

This section includes all the needlework stitches required to successfully complete the projects in subsequent chapters. The stitches are grouped into several subdivisions, such as embroidery or cutwork. Every stitch is placed within a technique that makes the most use of it, but remember that some stitches are used in more than one technique. Since it would be repetitious to include the descriptions of the same stitches over and over, you will need to refer to this section frequently.

Fig. 1–7 A grid is drawn over the design to be enlarged.

Fig. 1–8 The design is copied square-by-square to a new, larger grid.

Embroidery Stitches

Running stitch (Fig. 1–9). The easiest of all the stitches, worked from right to left. It is used as a decorative element in Kurpie embroidery and net embroidery and to strengthen cutwork. It may also be used as a tool in transferring designs.

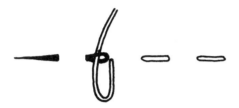

Fig. 1–9 Running stitch.

Back stitch (Fig. 1–10). Also worked from right to left, mainly used in Kurpie embroidery.

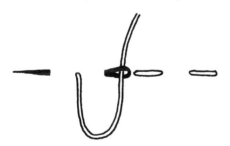

Fig. 1–10 Back stitch.

Stem stitch (Fig. 1–11). Worked vertically from the bottom up. It is used in Kurpie patterns and in cutwork designs to complete the stems of flowers and leaves.

Fig. 1–11 Stem stitch.

Chain stitch (Fig. 1–12). Worked vertically from top to bottom, incorporated into net and Kurpie embroidery and "snutki" patterns.

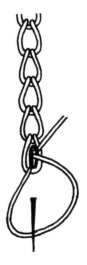

Fig. 1–12 Chain stitch.

11

Feather stitch (Fig. 1–13). Like the chain stitch belongs to the group of looped stitches in Kurpie designs. It is also worked vertically from top to bottom.

Fig. 1–13 Feather stitch.

Kurpie stitch (Fig. 1–14). Known by its Polish name because it is so typical in Kurpie embroideries. It is worked from right to left. The numbers and arrows marked on the illustration show

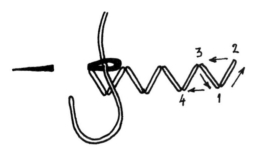

Fig. 1–14 Kurpie stitch.

the sequence of steps involved in working this stitch.

Satin stitch (Fig. 1–15). Used in net embroidery, Kurpie designs, and in several of the eyelet patterns to cover motifs that will not be cut out.

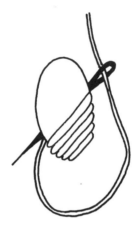

Fig. 1–15 Satin stitch.

Fishbone stitch (Fig. 1–16). Used in Kurpie embroidery instead of satin stitch. It is started with a vertical stitch, then angled

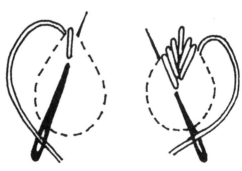

Fig. 1–16 Fishbone stitch.

12

stitches are placed alternately on the right and left sides. Each stitch is placed slightly lower than the previous one.

Cutwork Stitches

Overcast stitch (Fig. 1–17). Used in cutwork, eyelet embroidery, net embroidery, drawn thread work, and Kurpie patterns. It is worked from left to right, and each new stitch is placed close to the previous one.

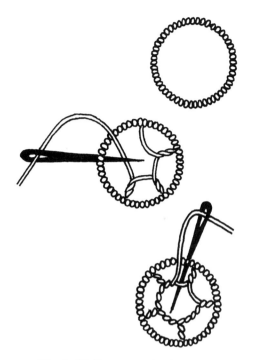

Fig. 1–18 Overcast wheel stitch.

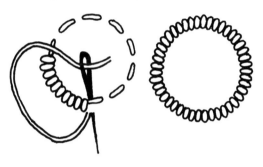

Fig. 1–17 Overcast stitch.

Overcast wheel stitch (Fig. 1–18). Used in some "snutki" patterns. The first step in completing this stitch is to overcast a round eyelet. Then make a series of overcast long loops in regular intervals along the circumference of the eyelet. After overcasting all the spokes but the first one, overcast the middle ring and then the final spoke. Secure the thread with a few stitches on the back of the work.

Buttonhole stitch (Fig. 1–19). Used in net embroidery, cutwork, and drawn thread work. It is worked from left to right. While working on cutwork designs, buttonhole stitches must be placed close to one another to secure what will become the edge of the motif.

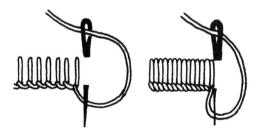

Fig. 1–19 Buttonhole stitch.

13

Buttonhole bars (Fig. 1–20). Used in cutwork, and created in two steps. 1. Cover the space over which a bar is to be created with three or four strands of thread. This thread has to be of the same tension as the background fabric. 2. Cover this cluster of thread with the buttonhole stitch.

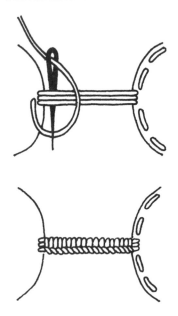

Fig. 1–20 Buttonhole bars.

Goldwork Stitches

Anchoring thread (Fig. 1–21). To anchor metallic thread, insert an unthreaded needle at the point in the fabric where the work is to begin, so that only the eye shows above the surface. Then thread the needle with just the end (approximately ½″) of the thread and pull the thread to the wrong

side. Secure the end of the thread on the wrong side with couching thread.

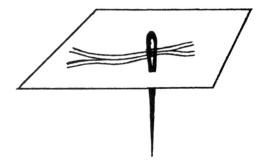

Fig. 1–21 Anchoring metallic thread.

Outline couching (Fig. 1–22). Done with overcast stitches placed at regular intervals. The spacing of the couching stitches is determined by the shape of the design. All curved lines must have closely spaced couching stitches so they retain the curved shape. A couching stitch should also be placed at each sharp corner or peak.

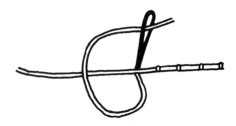

Fig. 1–22 Outline couching.

Couching with buttonhole stitch (Fig. 1–23). Attach the metallic thread to the background with the buttonhole stitch. This stitch can be used instead of the overcast stitch.

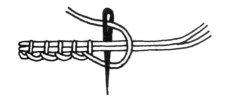

Fig. 1–23 Couching with buttonhole stitch.

Couching with chain stitch (Fig. 1–24). Tie down the thread with a chain stitch.

Fig. 1–24 Couching with chain stitch.

Couched open filling (Fig. 1–25). Used to fill a larger area of the design if the outline alone is

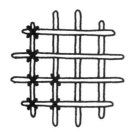

Fig. 1–25 Couched open filling.

not enough to complete the pattern. To form the filling, lay the metallic thread in a grid pattern and fasten every intersection with a tiny cross-stitch made with couching thread. Lay each line of the grid separately, then cut off and start and finish on the wrong side. After completing the filling, couch on the outline of the motif.

Flat work. A type of goldwork based on the same principle as outline couching, but here the couching is used to completely fill larger surfaces with metallic thread. Strands of metallic thread are placed close to one another and couched on to cover the background fabric. There are three flat-work techniques:

1. *Flat-work technique I* is sometimes called the turned-edge technique.

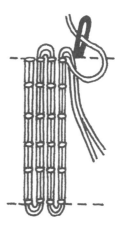

Fig. 1–26 Flatwork technique I (turned edge).

Here, the metallic thread is laid on the fabric in a continuous strand until the whole surface is covered (Fig. 1–26). At the edges of each motif, little loops are noticeable where the thread is turned for the next row. Those edges have to be covered later by outlining the whole motif.

2. *Flat-work technique II*, also called straight edge or clean edge, is achieved by cutting off and finishing each line of couching as if the work were just begun or ended (Fig. 1–27).

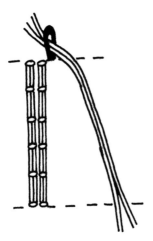

Fig. 1–27 Flatwork technique II (straight edge).

3. *Flat-work technique III* works well with modern metallic threads. This is a simple flat-work technique used for working

with metallic threads other than gold or silver. With this technique, the thread is laid in two consecutive trips through the motif (Figs. 1–28 and 1–29). The

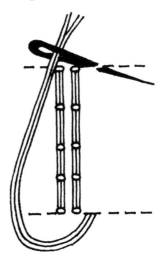

Fig. 1–28 Flatwork technique III, first trip through the motif.

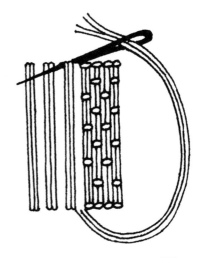

Fig. 1–29 Flatwork technique III, second trip through the motif.

thread is actually pulled in and out of the fabric, creating long stitches that are then tied down to the fabric with overcast stitches. The only precaution to be taken here is that the strands of metallic thread should not be longer than 13″. Otherwise they will start to unravel after too many trips through the fabric.

Decorative couching (Fig. 1–30). Achieved by placing couching stitches according to a planned pattern.

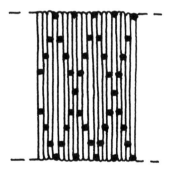

Fig. 1–30 Decorative couching.

Drawn Thread Work

Hemstitch (Fig. 1–31). Used in drawn thread work, hemstitches can be done in several ways. The work is done from left to right and each stitch is completed in a two-step procedure. First, the embroidery thread is slipped around the desired number of

threads in the fabric and anchored in the fabric. Then, while making the stitch, the threads of the fabric are pulled tightly together to form a cluster.

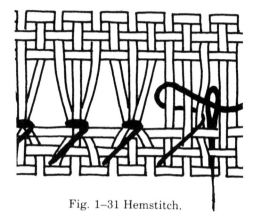

Fig. 1–31 Hemstitch.

Ladder hemstitch (Fig. 1–32). Formed by hemstitching both edges of the strip of withdrawn thread. The same threads on both sides are made into clusters.

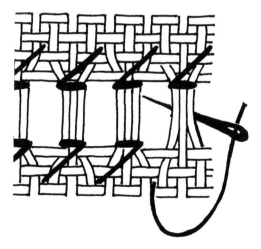

Fig. 1–32 Ladder hemstitch.

17

Trellis hemstitch (Fig. 1–33). Like the ladder hemstitch, the trellis has clusters on both sides, but clusters on one side do not correspond to those on the other side.

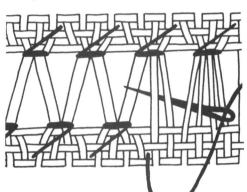

Fig. 1–33 Trellis hemstitch.

Single-crossing stitch (Fig. 1–34). Done on a completed strip of ladder hemstitch. The embroidery thread is pulled through the mid-dle of the strip by twisting each pair of ladder rungs.

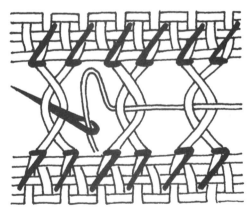

Fig. 1–34 Single-crossing stitch.

Double-crossing stitch (Fig. 1–35). Similar to single crossing stitch, but the twisting of ladder rungs is done in groups of four. First, the third rung is twisted with the first one, and then the fourth one is twisted with the second cluster.

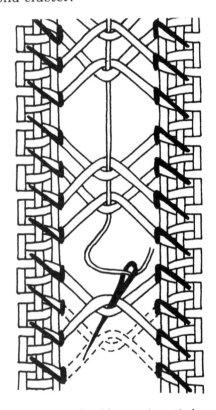

Fig. 1–35 Double-crossing stitch.

Lattice single-crossing stitch (Fig. 1–36). Used on relatively wide strips of withdrawn thread, it starts with the ladder hemstitch. Then in a distance of approximately ⅓ of the width of the strip from one of the horizontal edges, a thread is pulled through to create a single crossing stitch. The same distance from the other edge a second thread is pulled through to create another single crossing stitch, but a different set of rungs is twisted.

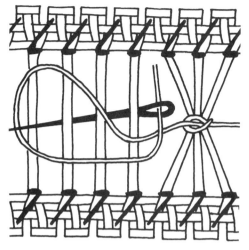

Fig. 1–37 Clusters with coral stitch.

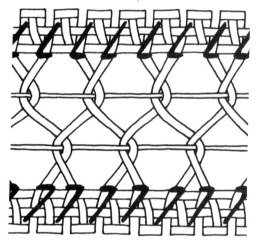

Fig. 1–36 Lattice single-crossing stitch.

Lattice with coral stitch (Fig. 1–38). Also worked on the ladder stitch background, but rather than placing the knots of the coral stitch in the middle of the strip, the knots travel from one side to the other, tying into clusters two rungs each time and each time moving forward by one rung.

Clusters with coral stitch (Fig. 1–37). Created in two steps. First, the ladder hemstitch is completed on the strip of withdrawn thread. Then the knots of coral stitch bunch together three ladder rungs at a time.

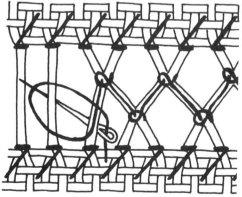

Fig. 1–38 Lattice with coral stitch.

19

Lattice with herringbone stitch (Fig. 1–39). Worked on two strips of withdrawn thread. The two strips are usually of identical width with a small section of fabric between them. This middle section is usually three to four threads wide. First, hemstitch the two outermost edges of both withdrawn strips. Then embroider the herringbone stitch over the middle section between the withdrawn thread strips.

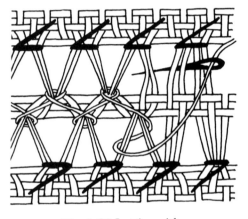

Fig. 1–39 Lattice with herringbone stitch.

Overcast bars (Fig. 1–40). Formed by overcasting clusters of vertical threads in a withdrawn thread strip. To make the first bar, anchor the thread on the wrong side of the work near the bottom edge of the strip. Then overcast three to four vertical threads from the bottom up. After the first bar is completed, pass the overcasting thread on the wrong side to the next group of vertical threads. Then overcast this group of threads from top to bottom with the same number of overcast stitches.

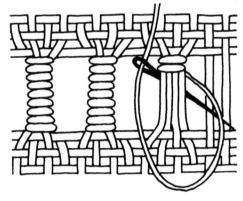

Fig. 1–40 Overcast bars.

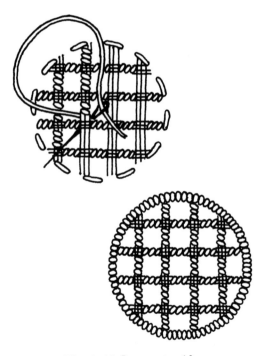

Fig. 1–41 Overcast grid.

20

Overcast grid (Fig. 1–41). Used to fill larger spaces of thread withdrawn at regular intervals, both horizontally and vertically. The remaining grid of threads is strengthened by overcasting, also horizontally and vertically. Each cluster of threads has to be overcast with the same number of stitches to achieve a uniform grid.

Woven spiderweb corner (Figs. 1–42 and 1–43). Used to decorate square spaces formed where two strips of withdrawn thread, one vertical and one horizontal, meet. The support for the wheel is created by the two threads used for decorative stitching on each of the withdrawn thread strips. These two threads meet under a 90° angle in the middle of the square. Two more diagonal threads are added to the wheel support, both of which join opposite corners of the square. Next, the thread is attached to the middle point where all the supporting threads meet and woven in a circular way over and under the support threads until you have a small circle (see Fig. 1–42). Then all the spokes of the wheel are overcast and the two raw edges of the fabric finished with buttonhole stitch (see Fig. 1–43). This is just one of the methods

of making a woven spiderweb wheel.

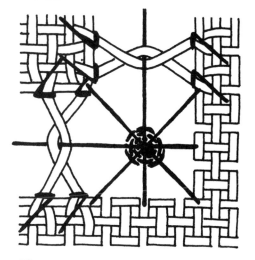

Fig. 1–42 Woven spiderweb corner with supporting threads.

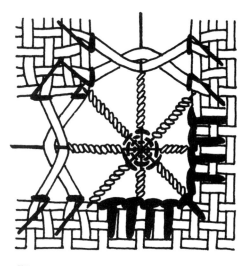

Fig. 1–43 Completed spiderweb corner.

21

BEADING

There are two ways of sewing beads to the surface of the fabric. Each bead can be threaded separately and then stitched down before the next bead is threaded and attached (Fig. 1–44). Or strings of beads, rather than individual ones, can be couched onto the fabric (Fig. 1–45). Couching involves working with two needles and two lengths of thread at the same time. First, anchor the thread with the beading needle in the back of the work and bring it to the right side where the first bead is to be placed. Then thread one or two beads and, right next to them, bring a second thread from the wrong side and use it to make an overcast stitch over the beading thread close to the last threaded bead. Overcast stitches can be spaced every two, three, or even four beads.

Sequins in all Polish folk designs are always attached by sewing a small bead through the middle hole of the sequin (Fig. 1–46) or by a knotted thread.

FINISHING TECHNIQUES

After you have completed the stitching, wash the piece of embroidery in a bath of mild soap. Never scrub the piece, but swish it around gently by hand. Iron the piece while the fabric is still slightly damp, by placing it on a soft surface, wrong side up, and ironing it on the wrong side. If the fabric is dry, iron it through a clean damp cloth placed on top of the wrong side of the work. When working with pile fabrics such as velvet or velveteen, it is better to steam the fabric rather than iron it, to prevent damaging the nap.

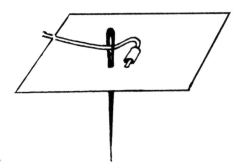

Fig. 1–44 Sewing
one bead at a time.

22

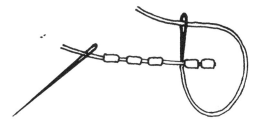

Fig. 1–45 Couching beads.

Fig. 1–46 Sewing on a sequin with a bead in the center.

BEFORE YOU BEGIN

To avoid costly and time-consuming mistakes, read all the instructions before starting any project. The description of each technique is included in the respective chapters, and the directions for each stitch are given in this chapter. General information about the technique is not repeated with each project. Some projects combine several techniques—for example, eyelet embroidery and drawn thread work—so consult both chapters before beginning the project.

Some obvious items, such as scissors, pins, and thimbles, are omitted from the lists of materials needed for each project. The materials needed for transferring a pattern to the fabric are not noted because they depend on the method of transfer you choose.

To avoid the time-consuming process of enlarging patterns, I have tried to provide full-size needlework designs for each project. Some are presented in sections because of space limitations; the instructions for the project tell how to complete the drawing. The diagrams for each project include measurements for a full-size item. The only pattern that has to be enlarged using the grid method is the Toddler's Overalls in Chapter 5.

Stitchery Tips

Overcast or hem the fabric before doing any decorative stitching. This will prevent the edges from fraying.

Before transferring a design, iron the fabric to guarantee a smooth image of the pattern.

To minimize knotting of the floss during embroidery, separate the length of six-stranded cotton floss into six individual strands. Then combine the number of strands you need.

Do not attach new lengths of thread to the fabric with a knot. Instead, make several stitches and leave a tail of thread and work it under completed stitches after you have finished the stitches with this strand.

When working with velvet, be careful not to crease the fabric. If you use an embroidery hoop, stretch a piece of muslin or other scrap fabric in the hoop and baste the velvet on top, without clamping the velvet itself in the hoop.

When buying materials for a project, allow for your particular way of working. Some stitchers are very careful with threads and waste only minimal amounts, while others may waste thread as imperfect stitches are pulled out and replaced with new ones. Some stitchers cover designs thinly, while others prefer heavy coverage. All these factors will determine the amount of thread needed to complete a particular pattern. It is usually better to buy more thread than you need, and any left over can always be used in your next project.

Plate 1 Traditional Polish beadwork on an antique vest.

Plate 2 Three
goldwork pictures
(see Chapter 2).

Plate 3 Floral bou-
quet in goldwork
(see Chapter 2).

Plate 4 Goldwork
picture frames (see
Chapter 2).

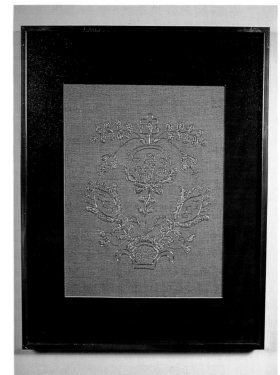

Plate 5 Beaded black velvet purse and belt (see Chapter 3).

Plate 7 Beaded makeup pouch and eyeglass case (see Chapter 3).

Plate 6 Bellpull (see Chapter 3).

Plate 8 Embroidered net christening dress (see Chapter 4).

Plate 9 Peasant blouse in drawn thread (see Chapter 7) and embroidered net doily (see Chapter 4).

Plate 10 Snutki doily (see Chapter 6) and three beaded jewelry boxes (see Chapter 3).

Plate 11 Cutwork collar (see Chapter 5) and beaded velvet wallet purse (see Chapter 3).

Plate 13 Traditional apron in drawn thread embroidery (see Chapter 7).

Plate 12 Redbird and bluebird pot holders, worked in drawn thread and cross stitch (see Chapter 7).

Plate 14 Drawn thread table runner (see Chapter 7).

Plate 15 Eyelet pil-
lowcases (see Chap-
ter 5) and drawn
thread sachet (see
Chapter 7).

Plate 16 Drawn
thread work pil-
lows (see Chap-
ter 7).

Plate 17 Toddler's overalls with eyelet embroidery (see Chapter 5).

Plate 18 Kurpie stitch on linen placemat (see Chapter 8).

CHAPTER

2

Goldwork

A BRIEF HISTORY

Since the beginning of history, people have been fascinated with pre-cicus metals and stones. That fascination has surfaced not only in many art and craft forms but also in embroidery. The use of precious metals gave the finished item an opulent look and was a sign of distinction or higher social status. So it is not surprising that the Bible mentions, for example, that Aaron's robes were decorated with gold wire. It is also known that the Egyptian king Tutankhamen dressed in garments embellished with gold needlework. In Europe and Asia, precious metal embroidery was at its peak for over 700 years, from the 13th to 19th centuries.

During the Middle Ages, the Catholic Church became increasingly wealthy and powerful, and this new strength was mirrored in magnificent works of art, among them embroideries, that were commissioned by royal-ty or nobility or made by devout parishioners "for the greater glory of God." These embroideries were included in *antependia*, the hangings for the front of the altar or lectern, or in complete sets of vestments, from priest's robes to chalice dressings. In the 15th century, a chasuble, or priest's robe, would be embroidered with gold, silver, and precious stones in floral or figural motifs. The embroidery illustrating scenes from the life of Christ, the Virgin Mary, and the Apostles, such as the Annunciation or the Crucifixion, was arranged to form the shape of a cross and often each scene was "framed" by pillars and an ornate canopy and embellished with floral elements. Most of the embroidery was done in a raised gold-work technique, with some motifs standing in relief against the background as much as an inch. Like many other works of medieval art, the embroideries often included figures representing the patron or donor of the item and his family.

But the Church did not have a monopoly on articles decorated with precious metals. From surviving artifacts, we know that gold embroidery was incorporated into wall hangings, screens, boxes, and clothing used in royal households and manor homes. In Elizabethan times, men and women wore richly decorated leather gloves with the cuffs and back of the hand lavished with gold and silver embroidery and often precious stones or pearls. Queen Elizabeth I had many robes embroidered with precious metals, and Mary, Queen of Scots, herself an accomplished embroideress, worked with gold and silver threads. Most Elizabethan designs were floral but often included animal shapes, such as lions, lambs, and pelicans, all of which had symbolic meaning.

Articles embroidered with gold and silver were so valuable that they were considered a royal gift and often were exchanged among the ruling houses of Europe. In the late 17th century, Polish King John III Sobieski received such a gift from the King of France, Louis XIV, a magnificent cloak of Chevalier of the Order of the Holy Ghost. It was made of black velvet and embroidered in gold and silver with a repeated flame motif, the symbol of the Holy Ghost. The cloak can still be viewed in Wawel Castle in my home city of Krakow. The same king is credited with stopping the deluge of Turks, who set siege to Vienna in 1683. This victory over the Turkish army was significant from the point of view of the needleworker because the victorious armies captured an incredible number of luxurious articles decorated with gold and silver needlework, which then created a vogue for Turkish artifacts. At that time, in both East and West, precious metal embroidery was used to decorate military standards, uniforms, saddle covers, caparisons, trappings and saddle bags, table carpets, and even traveling cases for spoons. Precious metals were often interspersed with pearls and precious stones.

Soon the fashion for gold embroidery started to spread far from the royal castles to the common folk. That explains why in the Kaszuby region of northern Poland, around the ancient Baltic port city of Gdansk, one can find rich, intricate examples of floral embroidery in gold or silver embellishing women's clothing, especially bonnets (Fig. 2–1), a practice that dates back to the 17th century. It seems that the rich, glittering needlework in that small area compensated for the bleakness of the cold climate. Embroidered clothing and liturgical items provided an avenue of artistic expression for the good folk of the region, and a large treasury of motifs served as a repository, to be adapted by needleworkers for designs.

Far from the Baltic shores, in the southwestern corner of Poland, em-

Fig. 2–1 Traditional goldwork pattern from a Kaszubian bonnet
(Collection of Regina Jaworski, Erie, Pennsylvania).

broidery executed in silver thread on black velvet adorned the bonnets women wore during Lent or when in mourning.

Gold embroidery was done by both men and women—professionals, semiprofessionals, and amateurs. Professional needleworkers, organized in guilds in the Middle Ages, earned their living through needlework. In the 13th and 14th centuries, some of the English professional embroiderers achieved such artistry in decorating liturgical items that their work became known as "opus anglicanum" (English work) and was appreciated and admired throughout churches in Europe. Also surprisingly, many of the vestments for Europe's medieval cathedrals were created by Muslim needleworkers in Spain, who blended Christian and Islamic patterns into true masterpieces. In many countries, nuns, who could be classified as semiprofessionals, also specialized in goldwork and often accepted commissions to execute different artifacts. Benedictine nuns were especially well known for the artistry and high technical quality of their work. They also tried to spread the knowledge of needlework by teaching it to the girls attending their convent schools.

In China, on the other side of the world, goldwork was produced mainly by professional embroiderers in imperial workshops or by the ladies of the leisure class. Precious metal embroidery in China decorated Buddhist hangings and banners and the robes of Taoist priests, members of the imperial household, officials of the military and civil service. It was also included in the decoration of rank badges—squares of embroidered cloth that, when attached to clothing, identified the position of an official within the bureaucracy. In China, precious metal embroidery was usually done on silk background fabric, which was completely covered with designs.

Chinese needlework influenced embroiderers in Japan, who in the 16th century produced elegantly decorated kimonos. Goldwork also became popular as an embellishment to the splendid costumes of the Kabuki actors.

GOLDWORK MATERIALS

In ancient times, gold embroidery was executed with thin gold strips or wire. Later, the strips were wound around silk or flax thread. In China and Japan, flax was covered with thin gilt paper and, in Cyprus, with gilt animal intestines. In the 16th century, thread was made by covering a silk or flax filament with a gilt strip of silver, while in the 17th century silver was substituted with cheaper copper. Apart from gold thread, often called *passing*, cord and bullion were also popular in gold embroidery. Cord was made by twisting several strands of thread together, while bullion was a name given to thin gilt or silver wire made into a coil, which could be cut to size and sewn on like beads.

Today, needleworkers rarely use thread made of precious metals. The metallic threads used today are made either by covering a thin layer of aluminum foil with clear plastic film, or plating a layer of plastic film with vaporized metal and winding the metallic fiber around a core of cotton, nylon, or rayon to add strength to the thread.

Gold and silver embroidery was usually done on velvet, linen, satin, damask, silk, and kid leather. These are still the best choices for the background fabric, which has to be a closely woven one. All goldwork projects are backed with cotton or linen attached to the background fabric.

All gold embroidery is done on a frame or a hoop with a wide-eyed needle and two strands of gold or silver thread. A second, thin needle is used for couching, done with a thin but strong silk or cotton thread.

GOLDWORK TECHNIQUES

There are three basic types of goldwork — outline work, flat work, and raised work. Outline work, or couching, is probably the simplest of the three and is done by covering the outlines of the motifs with an unbroken

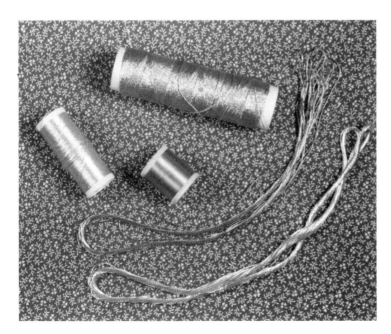

Fig. 2–2 A selection of metallic threads. The smallest spool in the middle is silk couching thread.

29

line of gold or silver thread laid on the surface of the fabric and anchored by small overcast stitches executed in cotton or silk thread—yellow for gold and gray for silver.

Flat work is based on the same principle as outline work, but the couching completely fills the larger surfaces with gold thread. Lines of laid thread are placed close to one another and couched on to cover the background fabric.

Raised work is executed in the same way as flat work, but as the name implies, before the motifs are covered with gold thread, they are padded with satin stitch executed in heavy cotton or wool thread. Sometimes a padding of felt, leather, or even cardboard is cut to fit the motif, which gives the embroidery a raised and sculptured look.

GOLDWORK PROJECTS

The interest in goldwork declined in the late 19th and 20th centuries, although it can still be seen in military uniforms and flags and in ceremonial regalia. Even in the Polish region of Kaszuby, women no longer wear

Fig. 2–3 A goldwork design adapted for embroidery flosses on a linen placemat.

30

the traditional goldwork bonnets. Nevertheless, such beautiful designs and interesting techniques should not be forgotten, especially when modern technology provides us with inexpensive, good-quality thread that perfectly simulates precious metals. Many of the traditional designs can be easily incorporated into embellishing wall hangings, evening purses, evening gowns, vests, belts, pillows, boxes, and Christmas decorations.

In Polish goldwork there is another creative possibility: Instead of executing these designs in metallic thread, authentic Kaszubian colors—black, olive green, sunny yellow, bright red, light blue, dark blue, and brown—can be used in the floral motifs, which in turn can decorate numerous items in a home (Fig. 2–3). The most characteristic feature of Kaszubian embroidery is outlining, which is always done to every motif with black floss in stem stitch.

Small Picture Frame
(Color plate 4 and Fig. 2–4)

Finished size: 5" by 7"

Materials

7" by 9" rectangle of cream-colored linen
5" by 7" padded mounting frame
Size A yellow pure silk thread for couching
Japan Gold No. 7 (1 skein)
Gold metallic thread
Embroidery hoop
Needles
Transfer tools

Instructions

On the fabric, mark the outline of the frame with running stitch. Then transfer the goldwork pattern onto the fabric in such a way that the heart

Fig. 2–4 Small picture frame.

motif is placed in one of the corners (Fig. 2–5). Next, stretch the fabric in an embroidery hoop and complete the stitching, remembering that the motifs are filled first and only then outlined.

After the stitching is completed, take the fabric off the hoop and iron it. Assemble the padded frame according to the instructions provided with the frame.

Pattern explanations

All the motifs marked with a grid are completed with couched open filling in two strands of metallic thread.

All solid areas in the motif are filled with metallic thread.

All motifs are outlined with one strand of couched-on Japan gold, or with two strands if the outline is marked with a double line.

All couching is done with one strand of silk thread.

32

Fig. 2–5 Goldwork pattern for the frame in Fig. 2–4.

Large Picture Frame
(Color plate 4 and Fig. 2–6)

Finished size: 8″ by 10″

Materials

13″ by 12″ rectangle of natural, unbleached linen
8″ by 10″ padded mounting frame
Size A yellow pure silk thread for couching
Japan Gold No. 7 (1 skein)
Gold metallic thread
Embroidery hoop
Needles
Transfer tools

Instructions

On the fabric, mark the outline of the frame with running stitch. Now, transfer the goldwork motifs onto four corners of the marked area (see Fig. 2–7). Place the fabric in an embroidery hoop and complete the stitching, keeping in mind that the elements are filled first and then outlined. *Note:* Not all the motifs are stitched identically, but rather they form identical pairs placed on the diagonal (see Fig. 2–8).

After the stitching is completed, take the fabric off the hoop and iron it. Assemble the padded frame according to the instructions provided with the frame.

Pattern explanations

All motifs marked with a grid are completed with couched open filling in two strands of metallic thread.

All blank areas of the motifs are filled with metallic thread.

All motifs are outlined with one strand of Japan gold, or with two strands if the outline is marked with a double line.

All couching is done with one strand of silk thread.

Fig. 2–6 Large picture frame.

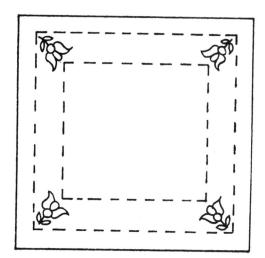

Fig. 2–7 Diagram
for frame in Fig. 2–6.

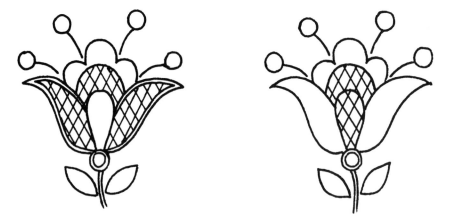

Fig. 2–8 Goldwork motif for the frame in Fig. 2–6.

36

Floral Bouquet Picture

(Color plate 3 and Fig. 2–9)

Finished size: 6½" by 7"

Materials

12" by 10" rectangle of natural, unbleached linen
Size A yellow silk thread for couching
Japan Gold No. 7 (two skeins)
Gold metallic thread
Embroidery hoop
Needles
Picture frame
Transfer tools

Instructions

Transfer the goldwork pattern onto the fabric (Fig. 2–11). Place the fabric in an embroidery hoop and complete the stitching, remembering that the elements are first filled and only then outlined.

After completing the stitching, take the piece off the hoop and iron it. Frame the piece yourself or have it framed professionally.

Pattern explanations

All solid areas or those marked with tiny dots are filled with metallic thread.

All motifs marked with a grid are completed with couched open filling in two strands of metallic thread.

All motifs are outlined with one strand of couched-on Japan gold, or with two strands if the outline is marked with a double line.

All couching is done with one strand of silk thread.

Fig. 2–9 The finished goldwork floral bouquet.

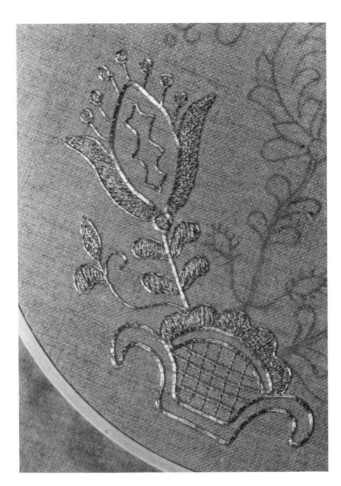

Fig. 2–10 Goldwork floral bouquet, detail of work in progress.

Fig. 2–11 Goldwork pattern for the floral bouquet in Figs. 2–9 and 2–10.

Three Round Goldwork Pictures

(Color plate 2, Figs. 2–12, 2–13, and 2–14)

Materials for each picture

5″ round gold-colored frame
6½″ by 6½″ square of brown velvet
10″ by 10″ square of cotton muslin for backing
Gold metallic thread
Light yellow embroidery floss for couching
Needles
Embroidery hoop
Transfer tools

Instructions

Stretch the backing fabric tightly on a hoop and tack the velvet onto the stretched backing. Transfer the goldwork pattern onto the velvet. After transferring the pattern, begin stitching the design, keeping in mind that the elements are filled first and then outlined. Stitch through the velvet and the backing.

After completing the stitching, take the velvet square off the hoop and place it in the frame. Be careful not to crease the velvet.

Frame the picture and cut off the excess velvet and backing from the back of the picture.

Pattern explanations

All motifs marked with a grid are completed with couched open filling in one strand of metallic thread.

All the blank areas are completely filled with metallic thread.

All solid areas are left open with no stitching inside.

All the motifs are outlined with two strands of couched-on metallic thread.

All couching is done with one strand of embroidery floss.

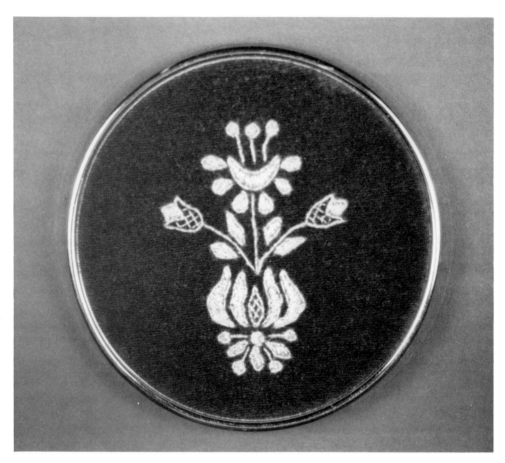

Fig. 2–12 Round goldwork picture, first motif.

Fig. 2–13 Round goldwork picture, second motif.

Fig. 2–14 Round goldwork picture, third motif.

Fig. 2–15 Goldwork
pattern for round pic-
ture in Fig. 2–12.

Fig. 2–16 Goldwork
pattern for round
picture shown in
Fig. 2–13.

Fig. 2–17 Goldwork
pattern for round
picture shown in
Fig. 2–14.

3

Beadwork

BEADWORK THROUGH THE CENTURIES

Beadwork is one of those needlework techniques that over the centuries has never lost its appeal. Collectors can certainly prize the beauty of pieces that even after 300 or 400 years retain their brilliant color and luster. In fact, in many cases the beads have strengthened the background fabric, thus helping to preserve the work in almost original condition.

The creative possibilities in applying beads and sequins were recognized hundreds of years ago by needleworkers who created wonderfully rich, mosaic-like effects in the robes worn by the clergy for church services and ceremonies, in clothing worn by royalty, or in folk costumes. Beads were made of a variety of materials, such as glass, precious or semiprecious stones, amber, wood, metals, pearls, ivory, pottery, shells, straw, marble, and seeds. Needleworkers devised many ingenious ways of piercing holes in the beads in order to attach them to the background fabrics. Stone beads and pearls were often drilled from both sides at the same time to avoid splitting the bead. Glass beads were made by molding or blowing, by winding hot, molten glass around a piece of wire, or by drawing hot glass into a tube and then cutting it into tiny pieces. These pieces were mixed with lime, charcoal, and sand, placed in iron containers, and rotated over a flame to smooth the cut edges.

The style of beads reflected the culture that made them. The ancient Egyptians seemed to be especially partial to faience, terracotta, and turquoise beads. Europeans during the Middle Ages lavishly used seed pearls, coral beads, and other precious and semiprecious stones, while 17th-century English needleworkers produced masterpieces with glass beads.

There were almost as many techniques of working with beads as there were types of beads. Beaded designs were used in weaving, knitting, cro-

Fig. 3–1 A selection of glass beads and sequins.

cheting, sewing, and plaiting. Designs could be created by sewing each bead separately onto the background material; by couching strings of beads; by using a tambour frame and attaching beads to the fabric with a crochet hook; or by stitching beads without the background fabric which meant creating a new beaded textile in a way similar to needle-made laces. By the second half of the 19th century, a machine to apply beads had been invented. This machine was particularly handy in the 1920s when heavily beaded flapper dresses became the fashion.

Beadwork motifs can be combined with other types of embroidery executed in silks, cotton or wool thread, or they might completely cover the background fabric to create stunning mosaic designs. The background material for beadwork was and still is almost always silk, satin, velvet, or linen, but nonwoven materials such as leather, paper, and vellum have also been used over the centuries.

In medieval Europe, beading was done on extremely costly fabrics, and no wonder since the beads used were equally costly pearls and gems.

Beaded motifs also were used to compliment gold and silver embroidery. In the 12th and 13th centuries, the most famous needlework workshops in Europe were located in Palermo, Sicily, and manned by Saracen needleworkers. They produced many church vestments and royal robes such as the ones worn by Emperor Frederic II of the Holy Roman Empire during his coronation in Rome in 1220. Even his gloves were embroidered in pearls, rubies, sapphires, and enameled plaques on the background of red silk. During the 14th and 15th centuries, richly decorated vestments and altar pieces were donated by the royal families to local churches or to the pope himself. One of the most famous embroideries of the 15th century is incorporated into the vestments of the Order of the Golden Fleece, which were worked on linen in gold and silk thread and encrusted with pearls, topaz, and sapphires. The embroidered figures included Saints John, Catherine, and Ursula, representations of angels, God the Father, and Christ. The painted pattern can still be seen where the embroidery has worn away.

Polish embroideries from the 14th and 15th centuries also conformed to the European fashion for pearls and precious stones. Documents from the 15th century include the names of the better-known embroiderers who worked at the splendid Renaissance royal court at Wawel Castle in Krakow. There Queen Bona of Poland herself oversaw the royal workshop of needlewomen, which, for convenience, was located close to her own chambers. The castle also boasted a second needlework workshop that employed only men. The men worked on large items such as dresses and church vestments covered with gold, pearls, and gems, while the women completed smaller items, such as fashionable small caps and belts, also covered with pearls. Pearls were usually first strung and then couched on. In the 16th century, the pearls were imported from Malacca in Malaysia. This was a century of prosperity for needleworkers in the Polish royal household. An embroiderer received an annual salary in cash, plus a certain yardage of fabric for his or her own use. If the king wanted an item finished on short notice, the embroiderers would receive a bonus.

The appeal of embroidery with precious stones extended beyond Polish royalty. From court inventories, paintings, and lists of New Year gifts, we know that Queen Elizabeth I owned numerous gowns and capes beaded with seed pearls and gems. Unfortunately the most splendid dresses, those covered with jewels, have not survived, for they would be dismantled as soon as they were soiled or went out of style and the jewels reused for another item. Queen Elizabeth I also wore jeweled gloves and slippers decorated with pearls and garnets, and she owned magnificent books covered in velvet, richly embroidered in gold and pearls. Seed pearls and precious metal sequins also decorated Elizabethan purses, bags, coifs, forehead cloths, and even nightcaps, usually exhibiting floral patterns and sometimes bird and insect motifs on the backgrounds of velvet, satin, or linen. Floral motifs were executed in multicolor silks and then richly outlined in pearls and sequins. On ecclesiastical vestments, strings of pearls were couched on to form elaborate foliage scrolls.

In Elizabethan times, glass beads imported from Venice were used in necklaces or as an embellishment on embroidery with precious stones. In the 17th century, England began to produce its own glass beads, and the second half of the century witnessed an extraordinary surge in the popularity of bead embroidery. Glass beads were usually couched with silk thread to leather, satin, and linen backgrounds. Beading was done either on a flat surface or over padding, which resembled the fashionable high-relief stump work. Often the entire background fabric was covered with beads to create the characteristic mosaic effect. Beading was used on scores of items, from pictures, pictorial panels, boxes, hair ornaments, mirror frames, and purses to baskets and candlesticks. By far the most popular items were beaded mosaic-like pictures, which retain their full beauty even today. They were almost always done on a white satin background with brilliant green, blue, purple, and yellow beads couched on to form scenes and figures. Biblical scenes were favored, but contemporary famous personages were also depicted. The person or couple was placed in the center of the picture with representations of the castle or manor house in the upper corner. The rest of the surface may have been covered with a whimsical forest of fantastic trees and flowers, among which roamed unicorns, lions, stags, and camels. The pictures sometimes included birds, insects, and coats of arms. The background was either totally covered or sprinkled with milky, opaque beads. Almost every element of the pictures was beaded, perhaps with the exception of hair and hands. Beaded pictures were displayed as works of art or were sent to cabinetmakers to be made into jewelry boxes, toilet articles, or writing implements. Needleworkers in the 17th century also used beads in knitting and in making baskets with flowers by stringing the beads on thin wires. Beaded flower baskets became popular again in the Victorian era.

Fashion in the 18th century also found use for beadwork with glass beads and precious stones. The vogue among wealthy women was the detachable stomacher embroidered with precious metals, pearls, and jewels. Embroidered aprons with floral designs or cornucopia patterns also be-

50

came popular. The embroidery was executed in metal threads, beads, and sequins on a light background. The most favored bead colors were red, green, and light and dark blue, and these colorful beads decorated handbags, waistcoats, and even baby clothes.

The 19th century, and especially the Victorian era, witnessed a boom in beadwork. New colors of glass beads were introduced, such as opal, ruby, turquoise, and amber, and in the second half of the century jet beads were invented. Strongly influenced by the 17th century, Victorian needleworkers created beaded pictures of hunting scenes, buildings, and elaborate landscapes. Beading was also popular on boxes, perfume bottles, bell-

Fig. 3–2 Crown ornament stitched with faceted metal beads, bugle beads and rhinestones.

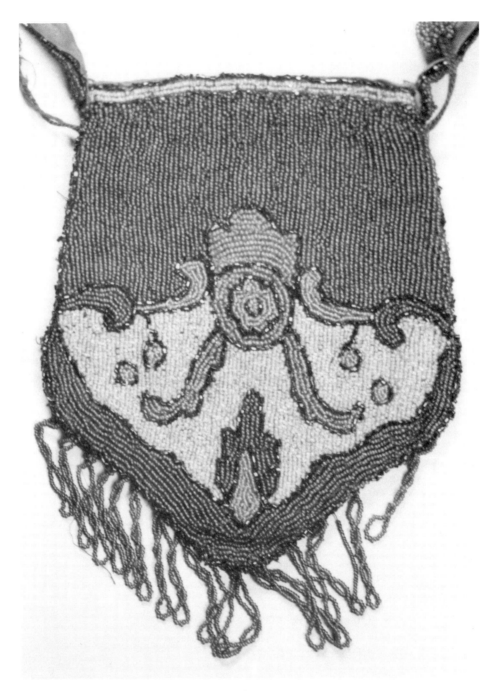

Fig. 3–3 Hand-beaded purse from the early 1930s.

52

pulls, wall tidies, bookmarkers, teapot stands and cozies, bags, and hand screens. Embroidery and beadwork often were combined; for example, the background of a bag might be covered with cross stitches and the design beaded. Victorian women also used beads in knitting and crocheting, combining glass and metal beads which were faceted to create a glittering effect. They also made samplers and used bead looms to make wrist bands and necklets.

Beadwork flourished in the 1920s, when the great couture houses produced whole collections of machine-beaded flapper dresses.

Beading was popular not only among wealthy Europeans and Americans. The Native Americans excelled in the art of beadwork. Before the colonial settlers brought glass beads to America in the 17th century, Indians made beads from shells, wood, minerals, and bone and had developed several beading techniques, such as loom work, bead couching, or the "lazy-squaw" stitch, which meant sewing several beads at one time in tightly packed rows. The motifs and color schemes in Indian designs were often symbolic and identified the tribe that produced them. The background material for Indian beading was leather or cloth, and the designs decorated war shirts, vests, leggings, moccasins, belt bags, and knife sheaths.

Beadwork was popular among the simple folk in many parts of the world and it found its place in decorating the clothing of peasants in Sweden, Hungary, and Yugoslavia as well as in many other countries.

POLISH FOLK BEADWORK

At the end of the 18th century, peasant women in southwestern Poland were decorating their silk bonnets with thin silver- and gold-colored tin plates in a variety of shapes, such as hearts, stars, and leaves. Small holes were pierced around the edges of the plates so that they could be sewn onto the fabric. The plates were arranged to form floral patterns (usually an elaborate bough with leaves, buds, and flowers growing out of a vase or a flowerpot) on the top of the bonnet and also on the long ribbons used to form a bow at the back of the neck. Later, round sequins were added for more glitter.

The 19th century witnessed an explosion in color, decorating techniques, and designs for costumes worn by peasants in Polish villages, and beadwork became one of the favorite techniques. At first the attempts to decorate with beads and sequins were timid and used only sparingly to enhance the designs or to underline the garment seams to flatter the figure.

As women gained more experience in beadwork and beads and sequins became more plentiful, the decorations grew more elaborate, often completely covering the background fabric.

The first sequins used by Polish peasants were made of metal, sometimes even of precious metal such as silver or gold, but later, glass sequins became popular. They were used as a decoration in themselves or to enrich other techniques. This evolution of the use of sequins can be seen on a variety of vests (bodices) worn by women in central and southern Poland. When silver, gold, red, blue, and green sequins became available, whole floral designs were constructed of nothing but these glittering circles. Sequins were attached to the background fabric either with a knotted thread or with small beads.

The prettiest beaded garments were created in central and southeastern Poland. Round glass beads were used for flowers and leaves and bugle beads for stems and geometrical designs. At the end of the 19th century, transparent colored beads were extremely popular. When attached to a dark background, these beads lost some of their brightness and created beautifully blended, mellow designs.

After World War I, some regions favored milky, pale beads, which created subtle effects, while others preferred translucent beads in bright red, green, yellow, blue, and pink. Sometimes glass beads imitating silver and gold were also incorporated for a richer effect. An additional decorative effect was achieved by combining beads of different shapes and sizes within the same design, or combining beads and sequins with colorful ribbons. The sequins were sewn onto ribbons and formed into a design, or the ribbons themselves created flowery designs while beads and sequins were added to enhance details such as leaf veins and the intricate interiors of flowers.

Favorite beadwork designs varied from region to region. Depending on the type of garment, whether a vest, jacket, or skirt, some motifs were designed as geometrical patterns or figures or stylized geometrical flowers. Some patterns even incorporated lettering that formed initials and greetings.

Floral designs of bouquets and sprays of blooms, especially chrysanthemums, pansies, carnations, daisies, roses, and large thistles, were the most spectacular of all. Depending on the region and the current fashion, each motif was either outlined or completely filled with beads of the same or contrasting color. A vest, for example, might be tightly covered with beaded flowers, and the embroideress prided herself in never repeating the same flower twice. Those vests, so popular around Rzeszow and Lancut,

54

Fig. 3–4 Beaded rose pattern from the back of a woman's vest made in southeastern Poland. (Collection of Regina Jaworski, Erie, Pennsylvania).

bore a resemblance to enameled armor and probably were not much lighter.

Because of the weight of the beads, the background material had to be sturdy. That is why beading was usually done on heavy silk, satin, velvet, or wool. But even then, only some items of clothing could be decorated with beading. The garments most commonly decorated with beads and sequins were women's vests or bodices, either sewn to the skirts or worn separately (Figs. 3–5 and 3–6). They were usually made out of velvet or wool in dark colors such as black, navy blue, dark green, and deep red. White was used occasionally, especially as part of a wedding costume.

Depending on the region, the depth of the necklines varied from high cut to low cut. The waistline might be finished with sometimes up to eighty pleats or flaps made of the same fabric as the vest and sewn around the waist. The beadwork designs were usually placed on the two front pieces and on the back and flaps, or they might be used to line the seams to

Fig. 3–5 Front of a girl's vest from Szczyrzyc in southern Poland. It is decorated in embroidery and beadwork done by a child.

underscore the slimness of the waist. Jackets worn in the fall and during cooler weather often had beaded designs along the edges and around the lower part of the sleeves, sometimes covering the sleeve from the cuff to the elbow.

In central Poland, around Lowicz, women wore handwoven skirts and aprons made of brightly colored striped wool. The skirts were finished on the bottom with a velvet ribbon, usually black, and beautifully beaded in elongated floral designs. Aprons were finished along three edges with a similar beaded ribbon. A short trip south of Lowicz around Piotrkow, women preferred to finish their striped aprons with a 2"- to 4"-wide strip of simple crocheting on which they beaded stylized flowers and geometrical designs. The aprons were black, dark blue, or white and decorated in a combination of techniques, such as embroidery, beading, and appliqué. Lace

Fig. 3–6 Back of the girl's vest in Fig. 3–5, showing a row of flaps sewn to the waistline.

trim was appliquéd on the apron, dividing it into squares and rectangles that would be filled with embroidered and beaded roses, violets, and corn-flowers. The petals might be embroidered in blue floss and the inside of the bloom covered in red beads.

In the same area, smaller and unusual beaded items of clothing also became popular, such as stockings similar to leg warmers, which were knitted with beads. The leg warmers, made of heavily beaded dark green or black velvet, buttoned at the back of the leg and covered the calf of the leg above the shoe and below the edge of the skirt. Similar to leg warmers were detachable cuffs, which were originally knitted with beads and later beaded on velvet with floral designs and sayings such as "Good Morning" or "Good Night" or with the initials of the owner. They were worn by both men and women and often were made by young women as a present for their favorite young men.

Fig. 3–7 A doll wearing a costume from Lowicz. The striped and decorated apron is finished along the three edges with beaded velvet ribbon. The skirt's edge just peeks out from under the apron.

Men's clothing also incorporated beading on hat ribbons, dickeys, and vests. Dickeys were mock shirt fronts, usually made out of dark velvet and heavily beaded, that were worn on top of a collarless cotton shirt under a jacket as part of a winter holiday costume. Hat ribbons, made of velvet and completely covered with beading, were sewn around the crown of the hat. But the decoration of men's clothing was not limited only to beading. In the southern region around Szczawnica, men favored sleeveless vests made of royal blue wool richly embroidered with floral designs in red, green, pink, yellow, and blue flosses and enlivened with a generous sprinkling of glittering sequins.

58

Small items for children were sewn from scraps of wool or velvet and decorated with ribbons, beads, and sequins. In northeastern Poland, mothers made little hats for their children to wear on special occasions such as church holidays or for trips to town.

Trips to town were made regularly so that the women could visit shops and buy embroidery supplies, flosses, beads, and sequins. The trips were often made on market days when a special open-air market was set up in the middle of town where the villagers could sell their produce and animals, and where traders in cloth, sewing supplies, and ready-made clothing set up special booths. The poorer peasants who could not afford the costly decorations usually got their few supplies from traveling salesmen. The women bartered with them for sewing supplies in exchange for old clothing. Occasionally, women used decorations from old, out-of-fashion clothing to make new items.

Young Polish women learned beadwork at an early age and prepared their own holiday or wedding costumes. The more talented ones set the fashion for the rest of the village and often helped their friends and neighbors complete the more complicated designs. This was considered a friendly gesture and no payment was required or expected. These young women drew the design on the fabric or drew it on paper and then transferred it to the fabric by basting paper and fabric together, but the extremely talented ones often simply created the design as they were beading.

BEADWORK TECHNIQUE

In Polish folk beadwork, beads can be sewn on one at a time or couched on. To couch the beads, you will need two needles and two lengths of thread. Thread one length of thread through an extremely slim beading needle, knot the end, and bring the needle up to the right side of the fabric where you will begin the beading. Slip the first bead on the thread and attach it to the background fabric. With the second needle threaded, cover the thread (but not the bead) with an overcast stitch. Place the couching stitch very close to the bead so there will be no visible space between beads.

To sew on each bead separately, you need only one needle. Thread each bead separately and attach it to the background fabric. Sequins can be secured with small beads or with small pieces of gold or silver purl.

Beading should always be done on a frame or a hoop, and you must be careful not to pull the beads too tight or the fabric will pucker when you take it off the hoop.

Makeup Pouch
(Color plate 7 and Fig. 3–8)

Finished size: 5¾" by 5¼"

Materials

Two 7¼" by 6½" rectangles of beige, 14-count aida cloth
Two 7¼" by 6½" rectangles of lining (felt, flannel, or floral print)
Turquoise glass beads (approximately 300)
Black glass beads (approximately 140)
White glass beads (approximately 150)
Beading and embroidery needles
Turquoise embroidery floss or pearl cotton
Sewing thread
A scrap of self-gripping fastener or two sew-on snaps
Embroidery hoop
Optional: 36" of turquoise cord

Instructions

Note: The cutting diagram in Figure 3–9 does not include seam allowances.

The broken line in Figure 3–9 shows the placement of the beaded pattern on one piece of aida cloth. Find the center of the pattern and the center of the broken-line rectangle and start beading following the graph chart (Fig. 3–10).

Beading on an even-weave fabric such as aida cloth is similar to cross-stitching. Each symbol on the chart represents one bead, which is sewn on with a half cross stitch executed with a beading needle.

After the beading is completed, hem the top part of both fabric pieces to form a tunnel for the cord. Then on the beaded piece, embroider a frame in turquoise floss or pearl cotton in buttonhole stitch. The frame is marked "a" on the diagram and is ⅛" wide.

Assemble the pouch and lining. If you are using cord, leave the two side openings of the tunnel free. Attach snaps or a self-gripping fastener on the inside of the top opening of the pouch.

Fig. 3–8 Beaded makeup pouch.

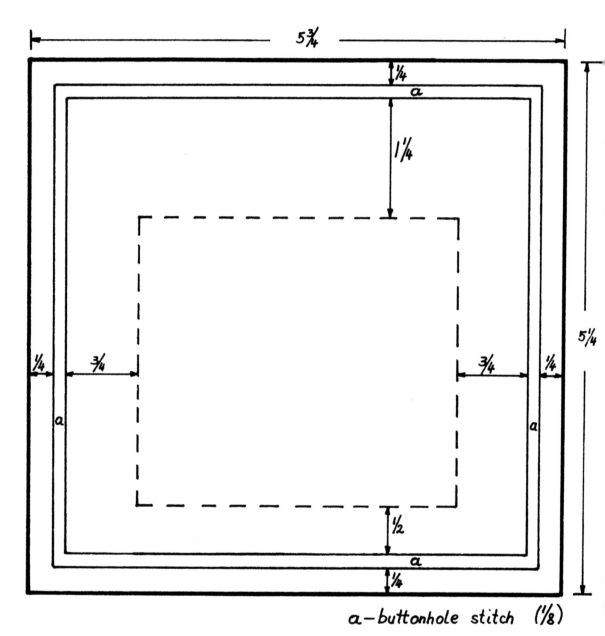

Fig. 3-9 Cutting diagram for the makeup pouch.

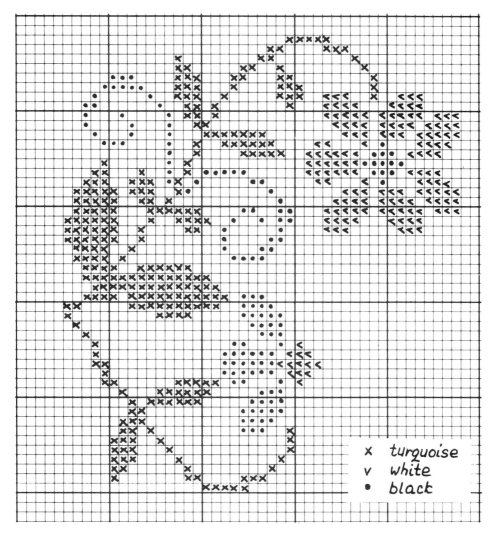

Fig. 3–10 Design chart for the makeup pouch.

Eyeglass Case
(Color plate 7 and Fig. 3–11)

Finished size: 3¼″ by 6¼″

Materials

Two 4½″ by 7½″ rectangles of beige, 14-count aida cloth
Two 4½″ by 7½″ rectangles of soft felt or flannel
Turquoise glass beads (approximately 600)
Black glass beads (approximately 310)
Beading needle
Sewing thread
Embroidery hoop

Instructions

Note: The cutting diagram in Figure 3–12 does not include seam allowances.

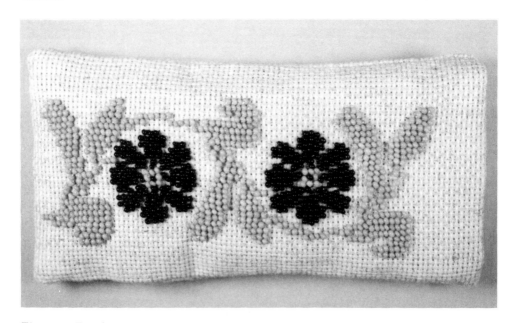

Fig. 3–11 Eyeglass case.

64

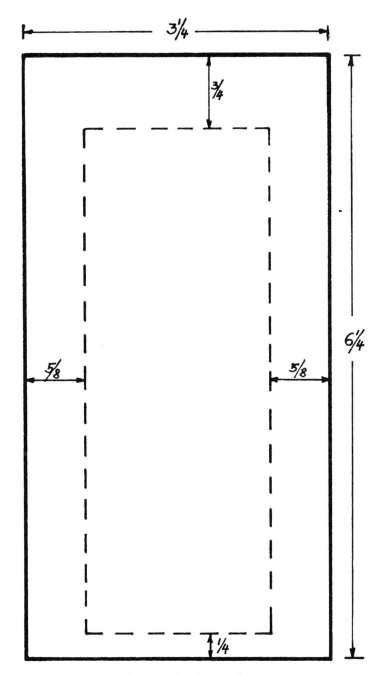

Fig. 3–12 Cutting diagram for the eyeglass case.

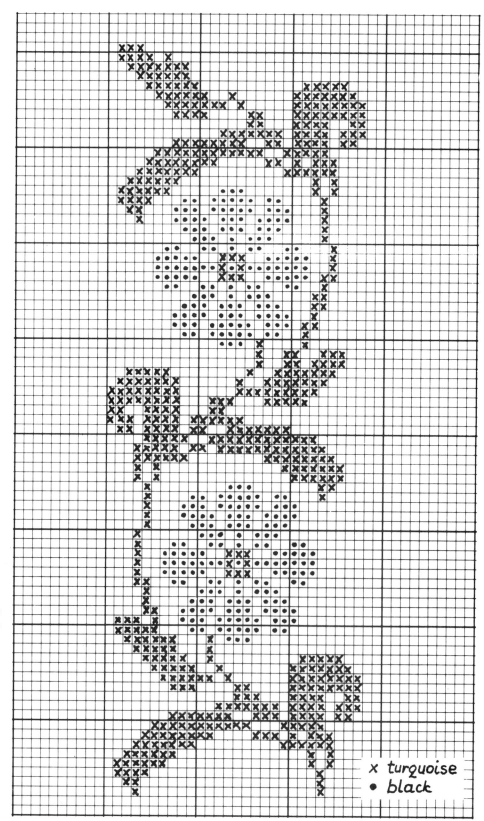

Fig. 3–13 Beading chart for the eyeglass case.

x turquoise
● black

The broken line in Figure 3–12 shows the placement of the beaded pattern on one piece of aida cloth. Find the center of the pattern and the center of the broken-line rectangle and start beading following the graph chart (Fig. 3–13). Beading on an open-weave fabric such as aida cloth is similar to cross-stitching. Each symbol on the chart represents one bead, which is sewn on with a half cross stitch executed with a beading needle.

After the beading is completed, assemble the case, lining it with felt or flannel, and hem around the top opening.

Black Velvet Sack Purse
(Color plate 5 and Fig. 3–14)

Finished size: approximately 10″ by 11¼″

Materials
Two 11″ by 12¼″ rectangles of black velvet or velveteen
Two 11″ by 12¼″ rectangles of black lining
Two 11″ by 12¼″ rectangles of muslin
5⅛″ by 9″ rectangle of black velvet or velveteen
5⅛″ by 9″ rectangle of black lining
4⅛″ by 8″ rectangle of cardboard
Black cord (approximately 70″)
Glass beads: gold, yellow, orange, white, red, blue, light blue, dark blue, green, dark green, silver, dark red, and pink
Beading needle
Sewing needle
Black thread
Embroidery hoop
Transfer tools

Instructions
Note: The cutting diagram in Figure 3–15 does not include seam allowances.

On the two larger rectangles of velvet, mark the pattern placement as shown in Figure 3–15 with a broken line. A small black rectangle indi-

Fig. 3–14 Beaded motif for the black velvet sack purse.

cates the center of design. Transfer the beading pattern to each rectangle. Place muslin on the wrong side of velvet. Place both fabrics on a frame or hoop, being careful not to crease the velvet.

Couch on the beads according to the color codes. For one rectangle, follow the color code A in Figure 3–16. For the second rectangle, follow color code B in Figure 3–17. Couch on beads to form a line of circles placed in regular intervals along the top of the purse.

To assemble the purse, follow the full-size pattern in Figure 3–18 and cut out a pattern for the bottom of the purse. Note that the pattern piece is cut on a fold. Cut an identical oval out of cardboard. Remembering to add the seam allowance, cut another oval out of black velvet and the third one out of the lining fabric. Sew the sides of the beaded velvet pieces together and sew the velvet oval to it. Sew the lining together in the same way.

Put the oval cardboard on the bottom of the velvet sack and slip the lining sack (inside out) into the velvet sack. Hem the top of the velvet and slip stitch the top of the lining to the inside of the sack.

Make two lines of stitching through velvet and lining to form a tunnel for the cord (see Fig. 3–15). On both sides, make openings in the tunnel and place the cord inside.

Pattern explanations

The color code is marked on the drawing with letters representing different colors.

68

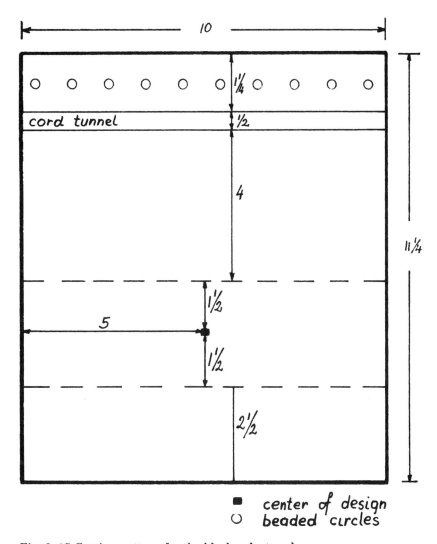

Fig. 3–15 Cutting pattern for the black velvet sack purse.

The double line represents the outline of the motif if it is executed in beads of different color than the rest of the motif.

The whole design is executed in round glass beads and the number of beads needed depends on their size.

The row of circles placed on top of the purse is couched on from a variety of colored beads. Almost every circle is different.

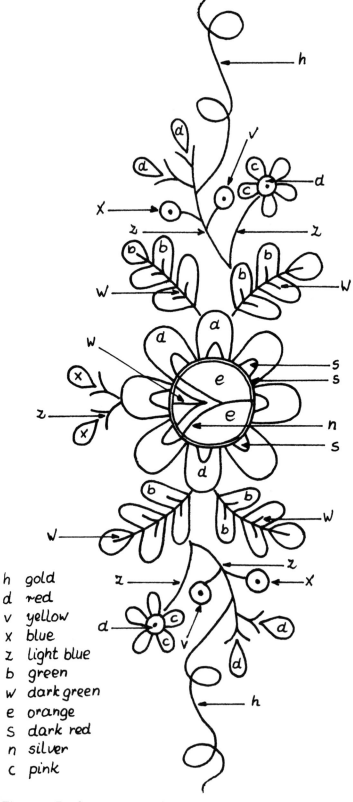

h gold
d red
v yellow
x blue
z light blue
b green
w dark green
e orange
S dark red
n silver
c pink

Fig. 3–16 Beading pattern Color Code A for the sack
purse.

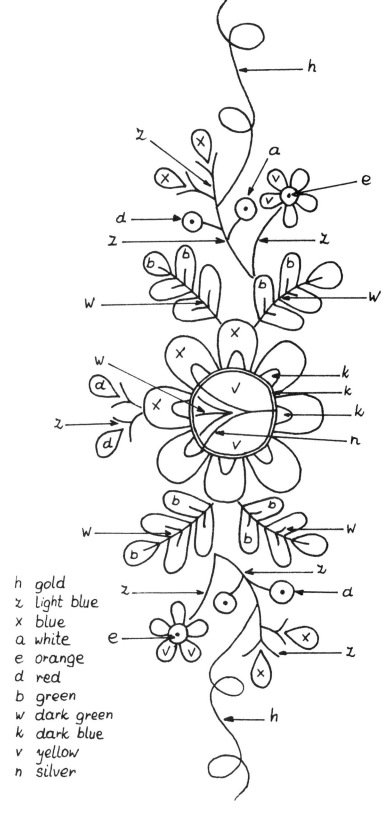

h gold
z light blue
x blue
a white
e orange
d red
b green
w dark green
k dark blue
v yellow
n silver

Fig. 3–17 Beading pattern Color Code B for the sack
purse.

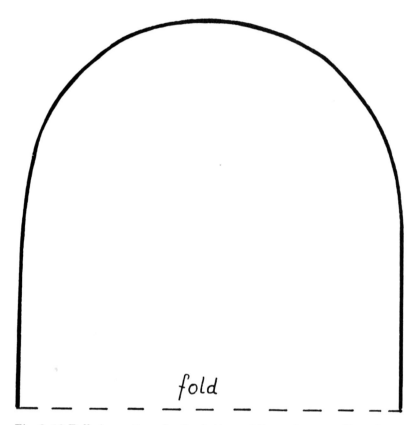

fold

Fig. 3–18 Full-size pattern for the bottom of the sack purse. Note that the pattern is placed on fabric fold.

Three Jewelry or Curio Boxes
(Color plate 10)

Materials for a 5″ Box (Fig. 3–19)

Glass beads in white, purple, light green, light brown, opalescent, and
    pink
7″ diameter circle of green velvet or velveteen
17½″ by 2½″ rectangle of green velvet
17½″ piece of ¾″-wide lace trim (off white)
17½″ piece of ½″-wide lace trim (off white)
5″-diameter wooden box, 2¾″ high
Beading and sewing needles
Sewing thread
Glue
Embroidery hoop
Small amount of fiberfill
Transfer Tools

Fig. 3–19 Jewelry box,
5″ diameter.

Fig. 3–20 Jewelry box,
4″ diameter.

Materials for a 4″ Box (Fig. 3–20)

Glass beads: white, pink, light green, and opalescent
6″ diameter circle of green velvet or velveteen
14½″ by 2″ rectangle of green velvet
14½″ piece of ¾″-wide lace trim (off white)
14½″ piece of ½″-wide lace trim (off white)
4″-diameter wooden box 1¾″ high
Beading and sewing needles
Sewing thread
Glue
Embroidery hoop
Small amount of fiberfill
Transfer tools

Materials for a 2″ Box (Fig. 3–21)

Glass beads: white, purple, light brown, green, light green, and opalescent
4″ diameter circle of green velvet or velveteen
8″ by 1¾″ rectangle of green velvet
8″ piece of ¾″-wide lace trim (off white)
8″ piece of ¼″-wide lace trim (off white)
2″ diameter wooden box 1⅜″ high (Fig. 3–22)

74

Fig. 3–21 Jewelry box, 2″ diameter.

Beading and sewing needles
Sewing thread
Glue
Embroidery hoop
Small amount of fiberfill
Transfer tools

Instructions

Transfer the beading patterns to the velvet circles. Place the velvet in an embroidery hoop, being careful not to crease the fabric, and couch on the beads according to the color code in Figures 3–23, 3–24, and 3–25, depending on the size of the box.

Fig. 3–22 A simple round wooden box for the beaded jewelry boxes.

75

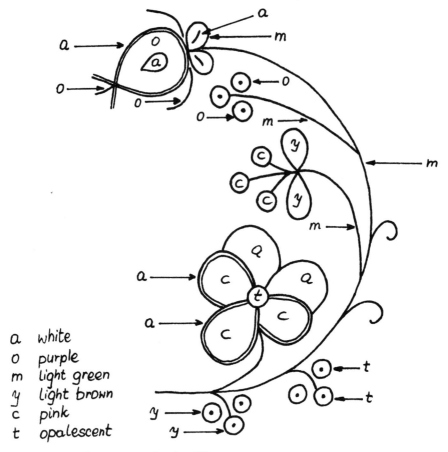

a   white
o   purple
m   light green
y   light brown
c   pink
t   opalescent

Fig.3–23 Beading pattern for the 5″ box.

Prepare the bottom part of the box. Attach the cover and mark how far the edge of the cover reaches over the side of the box (see Fig. 3–26). Take the velvet rectangle and turn the edges to the wrong side. Glue the velvet around the box, stretching it tightly between the bottom edge and the marked line. Be sure to use enough glue to hold the fabric securely in place. If the fabric extends beyond the marked line, the box will not close properly; if the fabric does not meet the line, there will be a gap between the lid and the sides when the box is closed. (*Note:* The side of the box can be painted instead of covered with fabric.) Place the wider of the two pieces of lace trim around the bottom of the box and glue or stitch in place.

To complete the cover, place the velvet circle on top and decide where to position the beaded design. Cut small notches around the edges of the

76

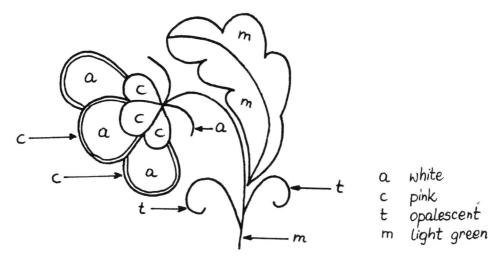

a   white
c   pink
t   opalescent
m   light green

Fig. 3–24 Beading pattern for the 4″ box.

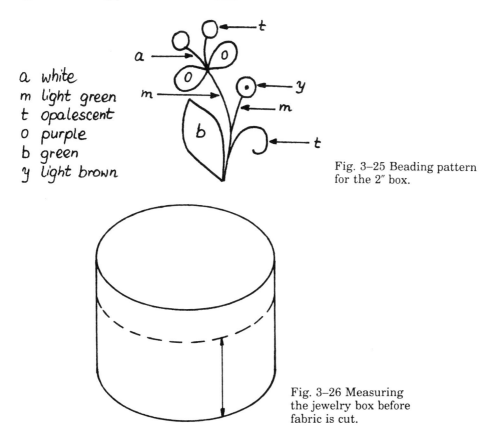

a   white
m   light green
t   opalescent
o   purple
b   green
y   light brown

Fig. 3–25 Beading pattern for the 2″ box.

Fig. 3–26 Measuring the jewelry box before fabric is cut.

77

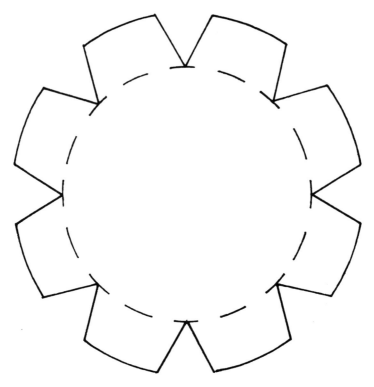

Fig. 3–27 The velvet for the lid of the jewelry boxes must be notched to form smooth edges before gluing.

circle (Fig. 3–27). Place some fiberfill on top of the cover, then place the beaded velvet on top to see if you have made enough notches and that they are long enough to easily glue the flaps to the side of the cover. If not, cut out more notches. The velvet should form a slightly puffed surface, so don't stretch it too tightly over the cover. Glue all the side flaps to the side of the cover. Adjust the fabric as you glue the flaps to prevent wrinkles.

Trim the excess fabric even with the edge of the cover. To hide the glued flaps, stitch the narrower lace trim around the edge of the cover.

Pattern explanations

The color code is marked on the drawing with letters representing different colors.

The double line represents the outline of the motif if it is executed in beads of different color than the rest of the motif.

The whole design is executed in round glass beads and the number of beads needed depends on their size.

78

Blue Velvet Wallet Purse

(Color plate 11 and Fig. 3–28)

Finished size: approximately 10½″ by 6″

Materials

12½″ by 18″ rectangle of dark blue velvet
12½″ by 18″ rectangle of dark blue lining
12½″ by 18″ rectangle of muslin
Two 3¾″ by 6¾″ rectangles of dark blue velvet
Two 3¾″ by 6¾″ rectangles of dark blue lining
10½″ by 16″ rectangle of cardboard
Glass beads: light blue, dark blue, blue, yellow, orange, red, green, light
    green, silver, white, purple, pink, black, and brown
Dark blue sewing thread
Beading and sewing needles
Embroidery hoop
Transfer tools

Instructions

Note: The cutting diagrams in Figures 3–29, 3–30, 3–31, and 3–32 do not include seam allowances.

Enlarge the cutting diagram in Figure 3–29 to the specified size. Copy the drawing onto a piece of cardboard and trim off along the top rounded edge as shown. Crease the cardboard along the fold lines. Center the cardboard piece on the 12½″ by 18″ piece of velvet and mark off the outline with running stitch. Center the beading pattern evenly from both sides of the flap of the purse and ½″ away from the top edge (Fig. 3–31).

Transfer the beading design to the velvet. Stretch the velvet and muslin together in an embroidery hoop, being careful not to crease the velvet. Bead the design through both the velvet and the muslin using the bead-couching method.

When the beading is finished, sew the lining to the piece of velvet and slip the cardboard form between the two. Then, line each of the two small pieces of velvet with the small pieces of lining, following the size given in

Fig. 3–28 Dark blue velvet wallet purse.

Figure 3–32. Fold each piece in half lengthwise with velvet on the inside. Slip-stitch the bottom edge together between "a" and "b" (Fig. 3–32). Then slip-stitch each piece to each side of the purse along the long edges "c-b." Figure 3–33 shows the side view of the finished purse.

Pattern explanations

The color code is marked on the drawing with letters representing different colors.

The double line represents the outline of the motif if it is executed in beads of different color than the rest of the motif.

The whole design is executed in round glass beads and the number of beads needed depends on their size.

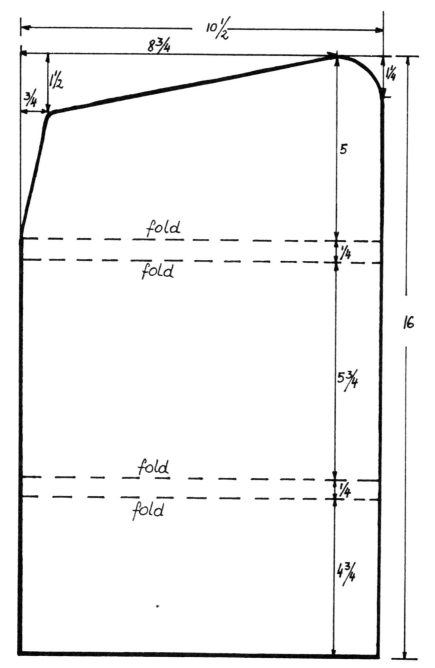

Fig. 3–29 Cutting diagram for the wallet purse.

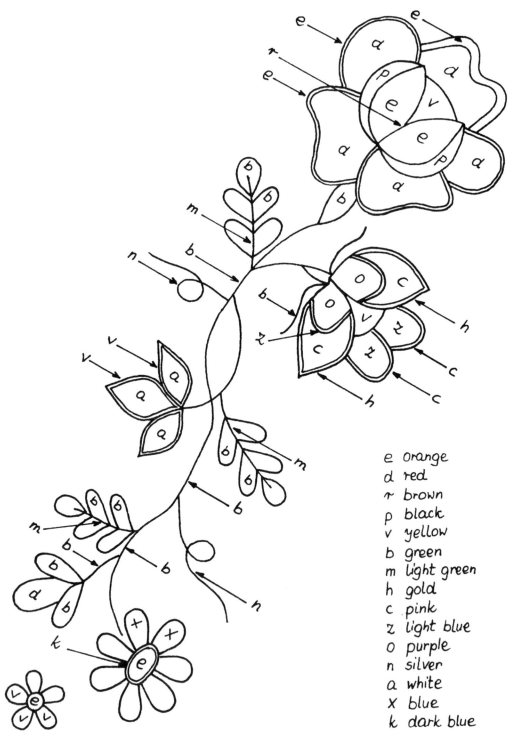

e orange
d red
r brown
p black
v yellow
b green
m light green
h gold
c pink
z light blue
o purple
n silver
a white
x blue
k dark blue

Fig. 3–30 Beading pattern for the wallet purse.

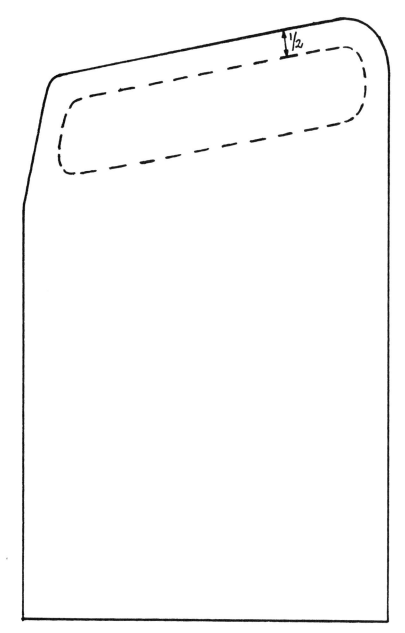

Fig. 3–31 Cutting diagram for the beaded flap of the wallet purse.

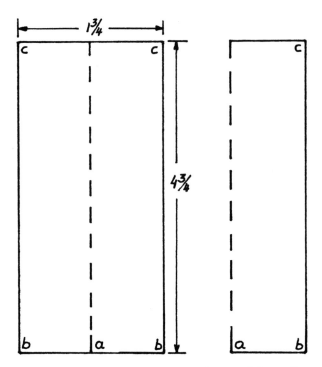

Fig. 3–32 Cutting diagram for the lining of the wallet purse.

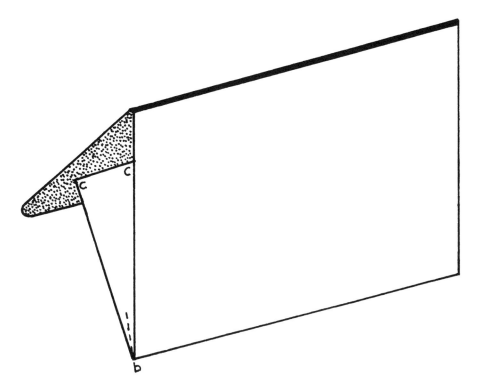

Fig. 3–33 The folded wallet purse.

Black Velvet Belt
(Color plate 11 and Figure 3–34)

Finished size: 29¾" long by 2¾" wide. *Note:* The belt can be lengthened or shortened by placing the beaded designs closer together or further apart.

Materials

3¾" by 30¾" strip of black velvet or velveteen
3¾" by 30¾" strip of black lining
2¾" by 29¾" strip of muslin
Glass beads: gold, red, pink, light green, light blue, blue, yellow, green, dark green, dark red, orange, silver, and dark blue
40" of ½"-wide black velvet ribbon
Beading and sewing needles
Black sewing thread
Embroidery hoop
Transfer tools

Instructions

Remembering that the seam allowance is ½" on each side, center and transfer the beading designs along the entire length of the belt. The design repeats three times: in the middle and on the two ends. Place the strip of muslin on the back of the velvet. Stretch the work on a frame or a hoop, but be careful not to crease the velvet.

Couch on the beads through the velvet and muslin according to the color codes. *Note:* The middle motif follows color code A, and the two end motifs follow color code B.

Fig. 3–34 Beading motif for the black velvet belt.

When the beading is finished, attach two 20″ lengths of velvet ribbon to the centers of the shorter edges of the belt, then slip-stitch the lining.

Pattern explanations

The color code is marked on the drawing with letters representing different colors.

The double line represents the outline of the motif if it is executed in beads of different color than the rest of the motif.

The whole design is executed in round glass beads, but the number of beads needed depends on their size.

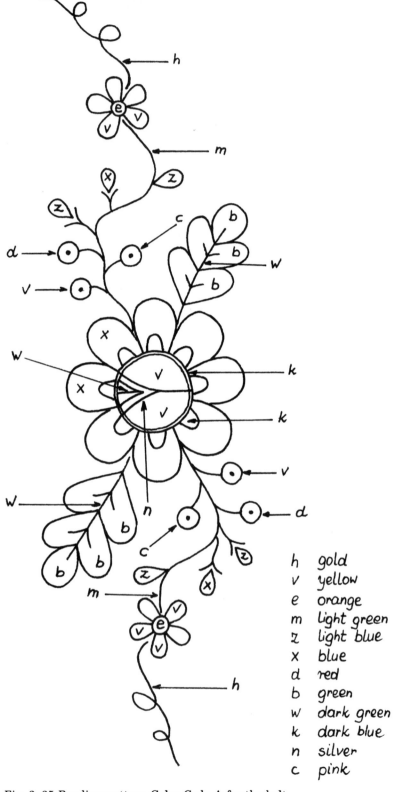

h   gold
v   yellow
e   orange
m   light green
z   light blue
x   blue
d   red
b   green
w   dark green
k   dark blue
n   silver
c   pink

Fig. 3–35 Beading pattern Color Code A for the belt.

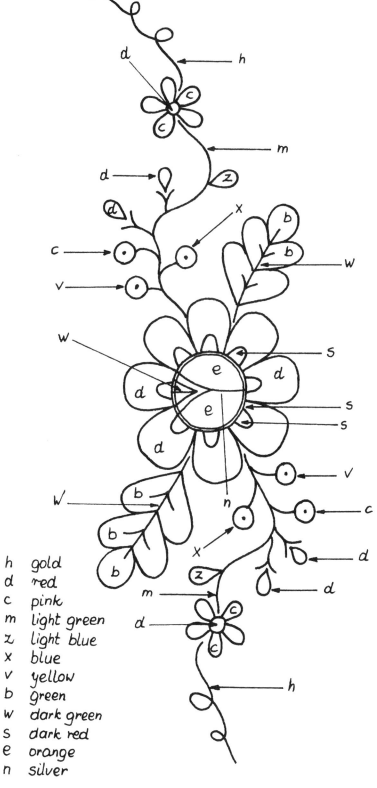

h	gold
d	red
c	pink
m	light green
z	light blue
x	blue
v	yellow
b	green
w	dark green
s	dark red
e	orange
n	silver

Fig. 3–36 Beading pattern Color Code B for the belt.

Decorative Bellpull
(Color plate 6 and Figs. 3–37 to 3–39)

Finished size: 34″ long by 2″ wide. *Note:* The bellpull can be lengthened by placing the beaded designs further apart.

Materials

3″ by 35″ strip of black velvet or velveteen
3″ by 35″ strip of black lining
2″ by 34″ strip of muslin
Glass beads: white, green, pink, red, orange, blue, yellow, gold, dark red, purple, dark blue, and light blue
Tassel
Beading and sewing needles
Black sewing thread
Embroidery hoop
Transfer tools

Instructions

Remembering that the seam allowance is ½″ on each side, center and transfer the beading designs on the whole length of the bellpull. Starting with one of the shorter ends, place the motifs in order, following the patterns in Figures 3–40 to 3–45 and ending with the grapevine pattern in Figure 3–46. Place the strip of muslin on the back of the velvet.

Stretch the work on a frame or a hoop, but be careful not to crease the velvet. Couch on the beads through the velvet and muslin according to the color codes.

When the beading is completed, stitch in the lining and attach a tassel to one of the shorter ends of the bellpull.

Pattern explanations

The color code is marked on the drawing with letters representing different colors.

Fig. 3–37 Top section
of the bellpull.

Fig. 3–38 Middle sec-
tion of the bellpull.

The double line represents the outline of the motif if it is executed in beads of different color than the rest of the motif.

The whole design is executed in round glass beads, but the number of beads needed depends on their size.

Fig. 3–39 Bottom
section of the bell-
pull.

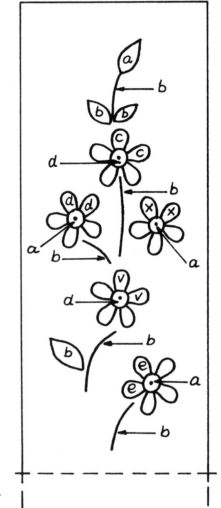

a white
b green
c pink
d red
x blue
v yellow
e orange

Fig. 3–40 Floral bead-
ing pattern #1.

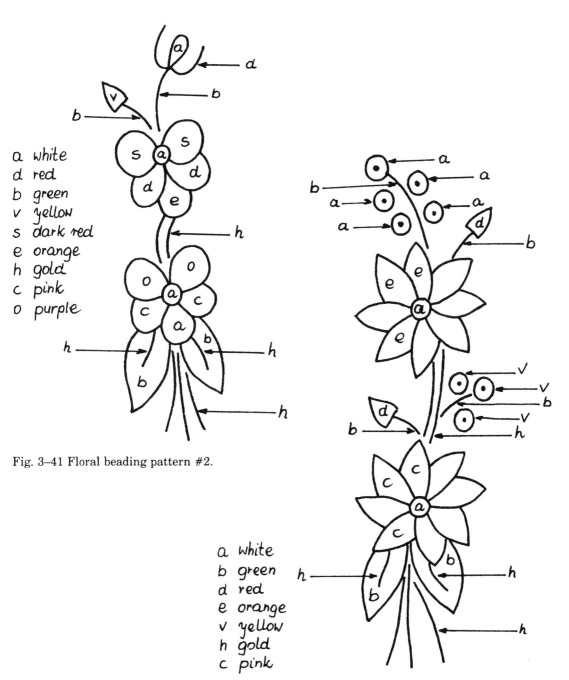

a white
d red
b green
v yellow
s dark red
e orange
h gold
c pink
o purple

Fig. 3–41 Floral beading pattern #2.

a white
b green
d red
e orange
v yellow
h gold
c pink

Fig. 3–42 Floral beading pattern #3.

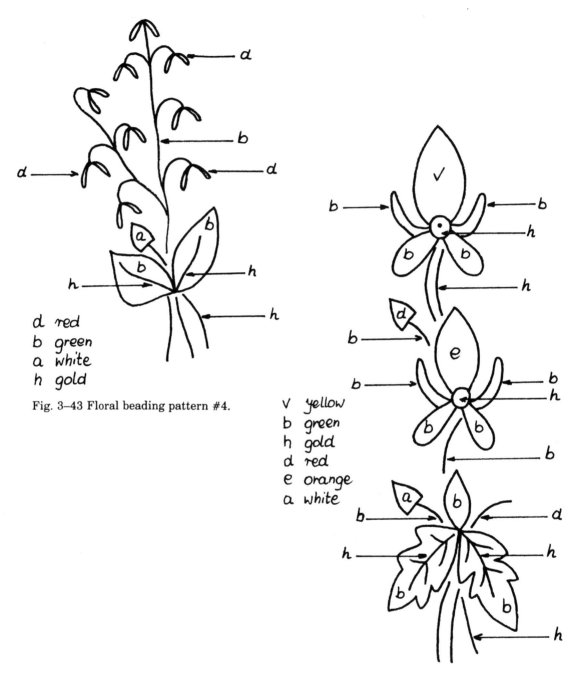

d red
b green
a white
h gold

Fig. 3–43 Floral beading pattern #4.

v yellow
b green
h gold
d red
e orange
a white

Fig. 3–44 Floral beading pattern #5.

94

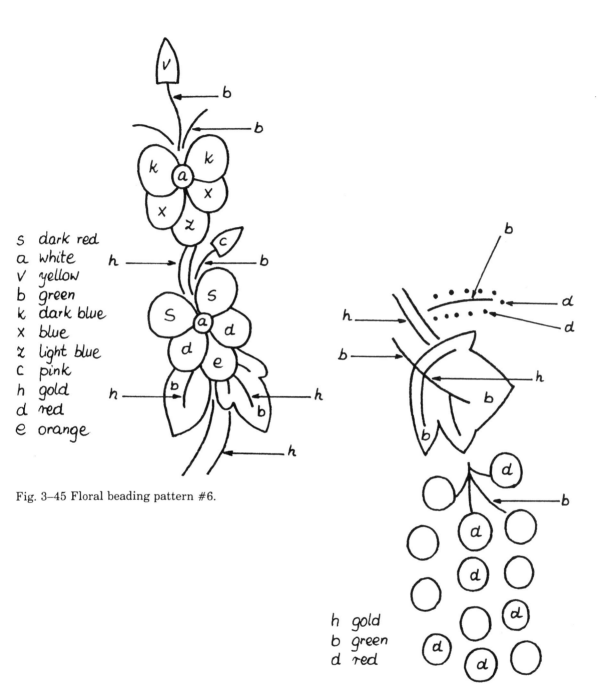

s dark red
a white
v yellow
b green
k dark blue
x blue
z light blue
c pink
h gold
d red
e orange

Fig. 3–45 Floral beading pattern #6.

h gold
b green
d red

Fig. 3–46 Grapevine beading pattern #7.

95

CHAPTER

Net Embroidery

A REVOLUTION IN LACEMAKING

Net embroidery is a fast and easy needlework technique that requires only a minimal knowledge of embroidery stitches but renders wonderful, elaborate-looking results. It emerged as a branch of lace production after net could be machine-made, and it has now been practiced for almost 200 years.

Until the end of the 18th century, lace production was dominated by two techniques: bobbin and needlepoint. But the invention at the turn of the century of a machine capable of making open-mesh fabric forever changed the lace industry. The fabric, in fact, perfectly resembled the handmade net background used in many laces. As the machines were perfected, they could produce nets of different weight with four-to six-sided openings. And soon, only specialists could distinguish between handmade and machine-made nets. Many lace workers began to use machine-made nets as backgrounds for motifs that they produced by hand and then appliquéd on the net. But net soon found other uses and was sought after as the ground fabric for embroidery. Since this revolution in net making, several techniques of working with net have been developed. The first and the simplest one is called needle-run and was perfected in Limerick, Ireland, and in Nottingham and the Isle of Wight in England. In these centers, the embroidery was usually done on a hexagonal-mesh net, where each mesh, or hole, had six sides. The motifs, such as bouquets and garlands of flowers and leaves, were first outlined in a simple running stitch woven in and out of the meshes of the fabric. When the outlining was completed, the motifs were covered with a variety of filling stitches that added to the richness of the lacy effect. Compared to the outline stitches, the filling stitches were executed in a thinner, almost spidery thread.

96

In Limerick, a variation of the needle-run technique also became popular and was known as tambour work (Fig. 4–1). Here, instead of a running stitch, chain stitch was used for outlining, and was often executed with a crochet hook and a continuous supply of thread. The fillings were also completed in chain stitch or in one of the more delicate filling stitches. Tambour work became popular in Brussels and later on was introduced by the British in India.

In Ireland, Carrickmacross also became well known as a center for net embroidery, and there two characteristic variations of this technique developed. One was appliqué and the other guipure (also called Renaissance embroidery), but only appliqué was done on machine-made net. To complete a design in appliqué, a layer of muslin was spread over a layer of net and both layers secured together. The design was outlined by couching on a relatively thick thread with a very fine one. Then the muslin was carefully cut away along the couched outlines and more decoration was added by using filling stitches on the net. Sometimes net embroidery was combined with eyelet work, and small round holes made with a stiletto were included to accentuate portions of the design. Net embroidery was usually

Fig. 4–1 Tambour work on cotton net.

done with threads of the same color as the background net—white, cream, or black. Few examples exist of net embroidery done in multicolored threads.

Embroidered net was used for blouses, collars, flounces, fichus, scarves, shawls, skirts, veils, and bodices. The motifs decorated the scalloped edges of the garment and were also repeated over the surface. Queen Victoria was fond of embroidered net and commissioned many items for herself and her daughters.

In the late 1820s in Ireland, schools were established to teach young girls the skills of net embroidery. More schools opened during the "potato famine" (1846–48), when making net embroideries was one of the few employment opportunities for women during those difficult years. Students were taught different techniques of net embroidery, net appliqué, drawn thread work, and crocheting. The teachers designed and supervised the work, helped with more complicated patterns, and later sold the work, often taking part of the profit as remuneration for teaching. Most of the sewing was done by the students at home after classes, with only the most delicate, most involved, and largest pieces done entirely in the classroom. The most talented students worked on these pieces, while the beginners and the less skilled students practiced decorating children's clothing or underclothing. Often the students worked on commissioned projects. Some of the students were as young as eight years old.

Irish embroiderers and lacemakers were called "the Flowerers" or "the Spriggers." They usually spent eight to ten hours a day at their craft, working in lace shops, lace schools, and at home. Their favorite workplace was the outdoors whenever the weather permitted. Limerick and Carrickmacross embroideries are still produced in Ireland, and the Flowerers still receive commissions from the royal houses.

In America, net embroidery was practiced as early as the 1820s. At the end of the 19th century, net was being used as a background fabric for beadwork, and beautiful bags were produced by sewing small beads onto net, each bead filling one mesh.

POLISH FOLK NET EMBROIDERY

In Poland, clothing made out of embroidered net became popular in the 19th century, and this fashion spread throughout the country, from the northeastern region of Kurpie, and the western part called "Great Poland," to the southern area belonging to Zagorzanie. We can speculate as to the reasons for the popularity of this technique, but two things we know for sure. Net embroidery had great decorative possibilities for the many regional costumes. Even more important, it allowed women to wear another layer of richly decorated clothing without covering what was underneath.

In almost every region, women decorated their bonnets with net embroidery. Some bonnets fit snugly around the head, while others were large and puffy, almost resembling chef's hats. Some were small pieces of fabric that barely covered the top of the head. Most of the bonnets were heavily embroidered and had two long (40″ × 8″) bands of decorated net sewn to both sides. These bands were tied under the chin into huge bows

Fig. 4–2 Side view of bonnet with bands worn untied (left) and front view with bands tied in a bow under the chin.

99

that looked like delicate, lacy butterflies. The bonnet usually had one central embroidered motif and several smaller ones placed around it, while the bands had motifs placed in strips. Bonnets were often made out of two layers of net—a delicate, small-mesh top layer and a coarser, larger-mesh bottom layer. The bottom layer strengthened the bonnet and allowed for the beautiful blending of the design and the background, rendering a delicate muted effect. Depending on the region, women wore bonnets only for special occasions such as weddings, christenings, or church holidays. In some regions, bonnets were a sign of marital status, and only married women could wear them. During the wedding ceremony, the bride's wreath of flowers, symbolizing virginity and purity, was replaced by a bonnet, a symbol of married life. This ceremony, accompanied by many sad songs and where only women were allowed to participate, was a tearful one as the bride gave up the carefree life of a girl and took on the responsibilities of a wife. The first bonnet was customarily a gift from the bride's godmother. Often the same wedding bonnet would be saved in the dowry chest to be used as funeral attire many years later. This beautiful tradition unfortunately prevented subsequent generations from enjoying these elaborately decorated bonnets.

Occasionally, especially on hot summer days, women wore embroidered net kerchiefs to church. On the kerchiefs, the decoration was placed in the corner that covered the back of the head and shoulders, where it could be admired by friends and neighbors. Smaller designs were placed in the other three corners, and the kerchief was edged with an embroidered border (Fig. 4–3). Kerchiefs were also used as decorative coverings for infants during baptism.

The mountain women from around Limanowa were known for their long cutwork or embroidered net shawls, which they wore over embroidered and beaded vests, and long net aprons with horizontal stripes.

Embroidered net was also used for making round, frilly detachable collars, which resembled Elizabethan ruffs. Some collars were made out of a 100"-long strip of net gathered to form a ruff. The edges of the collar were scalloped and in each scallop was placed a geometric or floral motif. Some collars were so large that they required wire skeletons for support.

In the 1930s, the villagers began to give up their regional costumes and to dress in the latest city fashions. Fortunately, net embroidery did not disappear but simply changed its form. Women used the old designs to create lacy doilies and trims for church and home linens.

Fig. 4–3 Embroidered net kerchief.

Several techniques were used to decorate net garments. The simplest one, needle-run, was based on the running stitch and the thread woven in and out of the openings of the hexagonal-mesh net. These designs followed the direction of the openings, either horizontal, vertical, diagonal to the right, or diagonal to the left. Some motifs were strip-like and usually made with one long strand of thread (Fig. 4–4). Here the embroideresses used straight lines and zigzags, called "crooked paths." Often, lines were used to join smaller motifs into one linear composition underlining the borders of motifs and the edges of garments. Central motifs, based on a six-pointed star, were called snowflakes or windmills (Figs. 4–5 and 4–6). Empty

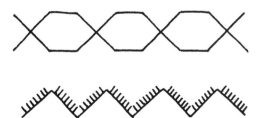

Fig. 4–4 Two simple linear motifs for net embroidery.

101

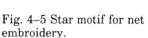

Fig. 4–5 Star motif for net embroidery.

Fig. 4–6 Snowflake motif for net embroidery.

Fig. 4–7 A sylized floral pattern.

areas between the linear borders and the central motifs were filled with tiny circles or minute stars. The artists also based motifs on squares, triangles, and parallelograms.

Needle-run, from geometrical designs, evolved into stylized floral patterns resembling twigs with leaves, twigs of fir trees, lilies, thistles, or the ever-popular bunches of grapes (Fig. 4–7). The women designed the floral patterns as they embroidered. To ensure the uniformity of repeated motifs, the embroideress counted meshes in the net in the same way as counted cross stitch. The thread might be carried under one hole and over the next, or, for straight lines, it might be carried over two or three holes at a time and then under one to make the sewing go faster.

As the art of decorating folk costumes evolved, new designs were created by combining buttonhole, overcast, and satin stitches. The running stitch was still used for the outlines and stems of flowers, but the lines were now gently curving. Instead of using heavy cotton thread to produce bold geometrical patterns, needleworkers began to vary the thickness of the thread to achieve delicate variations in shading. In the region most famous for its floral designs, around Zywiec, the favorite motifs were bunches of grapes with leaves, cornflowers, bluebells, and an array of imaginary flowers and leaves, all arranged along the scalloped edges of aprons, shawls, and cartwheel collars.

In many regions, floral designs were decorated with small round eyelets to accentuate the embroidered flowers or form separate motifs. In the more recent embroidered pieces, there is a noticeable influence of machine-made lace on the motifs used in net embroidery, and needleworkers often copy favorite patterns of store-bought laces.

Net garments were embroidered on a white net background with matching white thread, although in southern Poland, around Lancut, some of the embroidery was done in multicolored thread in soft pastel colors.

In at least one area of western Poland, pieces of net were appliquéd on the background fabric to fill larger motifs, creating an interesting contrast between the background, the embroidered motifs, and the net appliqué (Figs. 4–8, 4–9, and 4–10).

Not all women produced their own net items, but usually there was at least one woman in every parish, especially proficient in net embroidery, who would either make commissioned items or help the other women on their own embroidery. She was paid for her services either in cash, food, or exchange labor. She was also the one who created the designs, later copied

Fig. 4–8 Apron from western Poland decorated with embroidery and net appliqués. (Collection of Regina Jaworski, Erie, Pennsylvania).

103

Fig. 4–9 Central motif from the apron in Fig. 4–8 (Collection of Regina Jaworski, Erie, Pennsylvania).

104

Fig. 4–10 Motifs on the apron ties in Fig. 4–8 (Collection of Regina Jaworski, Erie, Pennsylvania).

by other women. Because of this arrangement, a great similarity in motifs and designs can be noticed within the same parish. Some embroidery was done by women who were not strong enough to work in the fields or who were too poor to own or rent land. Some areas became so renowned for their beautiful embroidery that the village women would receive commissions from neighboring parishes.

Because net garments required delicate care, there was usually one woman in the village who washed, starched, and ironed the garments for her friends and neighbors.

NET EMBROIDERY TECHNIQUE

All the projects in this chapter are executed on hexagonal (six-sided) nylon net (called tulle or English net), which is available in fabric stores specializing in bridal fabrics (Fig. 4–11). The embroidery is done with white pearl cotton No. 8 or with embroidery floss.

The first step in net embroidery is to copy the pattern onto a sheet of sturdy tracing paper. The outlines should be traced with a marker so that after the net is placed over the design, the drawing will not rub off and soil the net. When working with geometrical designs, carefully place the net over the design so that the central line of the pattern aligns with a row of holes. Pin the net and paper together and place them securely in a hoop. Baste both layers together and remove the pins. Instead of tracing paper, you can use light-colored batiste or muslin.

To begin work, thread a crewel embroidery needle with a 40" strand of pearl cotton. Instead of knotting the end, tie it securely to one of the bars of

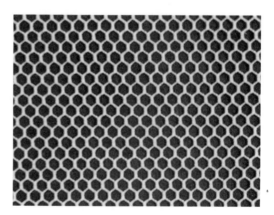

Fig. 4–11 Hexagonal nylon net, called tulle or English net.

net where the embroidery is to begin. The design is based on a continuous journey of the thread, so study the sequence in completing each part of a motif before you begin. When the motif is finished, or when the thread nears the end, secure the thread in the back by weaving over the ground already covered, or tie a new thread to its end. Weave with a running stitch by going over and under each mesh, following the pattern under the net. Always be careful not to pierce the paper with the needle.

With geometrical designs, all the parts of the same motif—for instance, the points of the star—must be the same size. To do this, count the holes just as you would count crosses in counted cross stitch (Fig. 4–12). When you have completed one section of a continuous strip of design, go on to the next section, carefully aligning both sections before you begin. With geometrical designs, you can simply guide the needle by counting the mesh (holes) of the net rather than following the pattern. This is an easy and fast procedure because with repeated designs you will quickly memorize the mesh count and not have to consult the chart. Polish embroideresses relied on this counting method, and it is the one I used when I embroidered the skirt for the christening dress in this chapter.

Floral patterns do not follow the structure of the net, so you don't have to align the row of holes to the design. Transferring the design is done in the same way as geometrical patterns.

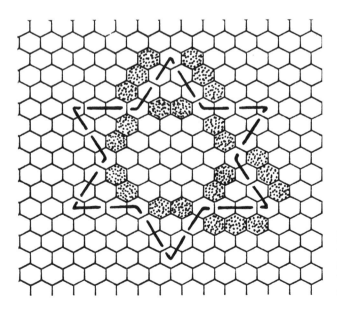

Fig. 4–12 To make sure all the elements of a geometrical motif are even, count the meshes (marked with dots).

107

The embroidery is done with embroidery floss, using two or four strands at a time for outlining and one strand for filling stitches.

When working with two strands of floss at a time a neat method of commencing the work can be used. Cut a double length of thread needed and fold it in half. Folded thread forms a little loop on one of its ends. Now, thread the loop through the needle, and slip the needle under the bar of the net and then through the floss loop. The thread, when pulled, will be invisibly attached to the bar.

Fig. 4–13 Outlining is done in running stitch a little to the outside of the line of the pattern.

The next step is to cover all the outlines in running stitch with a continuous line of thread. As with geometrical motifs, you may have to go over some parts of the pattern twice. The outlining should be done slightly to the outside edge of the pattern (Fig. 4–13). Again, be careful not to pierce the paper pattern. As you do the outlining, complete all the eyelets with buttonhole or overcast stitch (see the instructions for making eyelets in Chapter 5).

After completing the outlining, separate the net from the drawing and place it in a hoop. Complete the filling stitches using a thread thinner than the outlining thread (Fig. 4–14). When working filling stitches, estimate the length of the thread for finishing each row. Never use a new length of thread within the row. The thread should always end where it can be covered by the outline.

Proper thread tension is important in all net embroidery. The thread woven through net stretched on a hoop should be of the same tension as the net. If the thread is too slack, the design will be distorted. If the thread is too tight, it will pull and possibly damage the net.

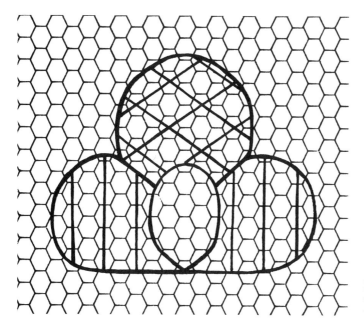

Fig. 4–14 Floral motif outlined and filled with running stitches.

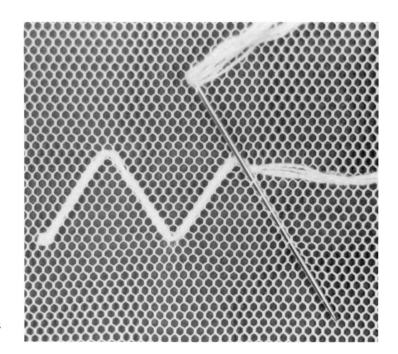

Fig. 4–15 Correct thread tension.

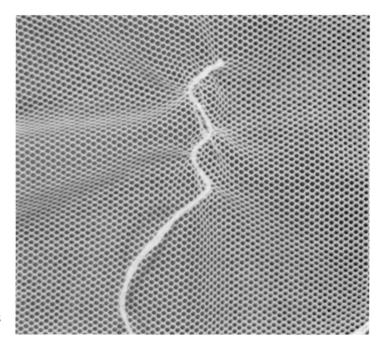

Fig. 4–16 Incorrect thread tension.

110

Floral Picture on Tulle
(Fig. 4–17)

Finished size: approximately 9″ by 5″

Materials

20″ by 17″ rectangle of hexagonal net
20″ by 17″ rectangle of plain or floral-print cotton background fabric
20″ by 17″ rectangle of muslin
White embroidery floss (one skein)
Needles
Basting thread
Embroidery hoop
Small picture frame
Transfer tools

Fig. 4–17 Floral picture on tulle.

Instructions

Transfer the motifs in Figures 4–18 and 4–19 onto the muslin rectangle. (I placed the two flowers 5″ apart, measuring from stem to stem.) Place the net over the muslin and baste together, taking care not to cross any lines of design with basting lines. Stretch both layers in a hoop. Cover all the outlines of the design with running stitch in two strands of floss. Stitch only through the net, not through the muslin. *Note:* You may have to go

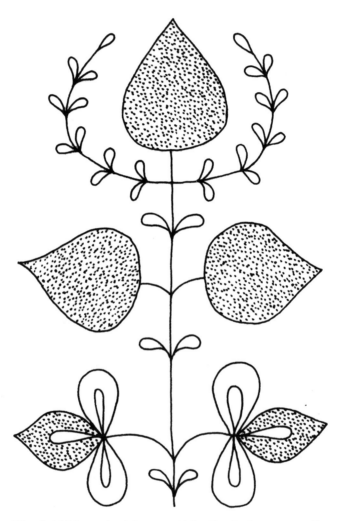

Fig. 4–18 Net embroidery motif for floral picture on tulle.

112

over some elements of the design twice. After finishing the outlining, use filling stitches such as running stitch and feather stitch to shade some of the petals and leaves. Do the filling in one strand of embroidery floss.

After the embroidery is completed, take the work off the hoop and remove the basting stitches. Wash and lightly iron the piece before framing.

Pattern explanations

All the dotted areas are to be decorated with stitches of your choice.

Fig. 4–19 Second net embroidery motif for floral picture.

Christening Dress

(Color plate 8 and Figs. 4–20 and 4–21)

Materials

Any pattern for a christening dress
Fabric and materials recommended in the pattern
Piece of net somewhat larger than the size of the skirt of the dress (I used a
    54″ by 38″ rectangle of net)
White pearl cotton No. 8
Piece of muslin the same size as the net
Basting thread
Needles
Embroidery hoop
Transfer tools

Instructions

Make a drawing of the complete net-embroidery design. Follow the diagram in Figure 4–22 and place each motif in its proper place. (The separate motifs are shown full size in Figure 4–23.) Adjust the width and length of the skirt by adding or subtracting motifs.

Transfer the design onto the muslin. Carefully spread the net over the muslin and baste together, being careful not to cross any lines of design with basting lines. Leave at least an inch of excess net beyond the edge of the scallops. Stretch both layers in a hoop. Cover all the outlines with running stitch in one strand of pearl cotton, remembering to line up a row of holes with each section of motif. Stitch only through the net, not through the muslin.

Outline the outer scallops with running stitch, then cover them with buttonhole stitch. Complete the individual motifs with one continuous strand of thread, going over the details twice if necessary. After finishing one section of the design, move the hoop to the next position. *Note:* The design can also be worked by counting the meshes in the net.

When the embroidery is completed, remove the basting stitches, wash the net, and trim the excess along the scalloped edge (Fig. 4–24). Be careful not to cut the thread that forms the buttonhole stitch. Assemble the christening dress and add the embroidered net as the top layer of the skirt.

114

Fig. 4–20 Central
section of the net
embroidery for the
christening dress.

115

Fig. 4–21 Close-up of the net-embroidery motif for the christening dress.

116

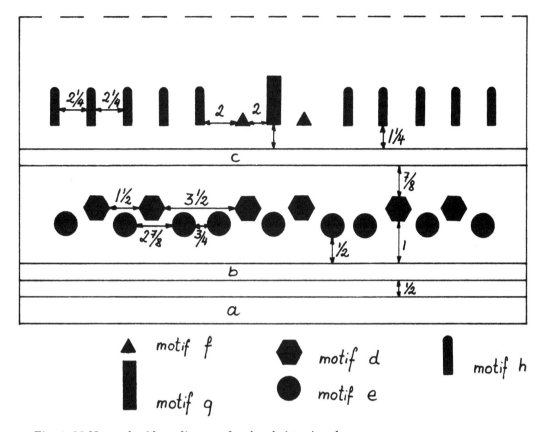

Fig. 4–22 Net embroidery diagram for the christening dress.

Fig. 4–23 Full-size motifs for the christening dress. The lettered motifs correspond to the embroidery diagram in Fig. 4–22.

118

Fig. 4–24 The excess net is trimmed close to the completed stitching.

Embroidered Net Doily

(Color plate 9 and Fig. 4–25)

Finished size: 12″ in diameter

Materials

16″ by 16″ square of hexagonal net
16″ by 16″ square of muslin
White embroidery floss
Basting thread
Needles
Embroidery hoop
Transfer tools
Stiletto (optional)

Instructions

The floral pattern in Figure 4–26 represents only half of the design. Make a drawing of an entire design for the doily. When the drawing is completed, motif "a" of the first half will be placed next to motif "b" of the second half (Fig. 4–26). Also complete the drawing of the scallops (the pattern in Figure 4–27 shows one-quarter of the design). Combine the two drawings by fitting the floral pattern within the circle of scallops.

Transfer the design to a piece of muslin. Spread the net over the muslin and baste together, taking care not to cross any lines of design with basting lines. Stretch both layers in a hoop.

Cover the outline of the floral design in running stitch with two strands of embroidery floss. Stitch only through the net and not through the muslin. After completing the outlining, use a running filling stitch in one strand of embroidery floss to shade petals and leaves marked on the pattern with dots.

Reposition the net and muslin in the hoop and make the scallops. The outer edge of the scallops is covered in buttonhole stitch in three strands of floss at a time; outline the inside scallops in running stitch. Fill in the scallops with running stitch in one strand of floss. After completing the embroidery, take the net and muslin off the hoop and remove the basting stitches. Trim excess net along the edges of the scallops. Wash, lightly starch, and iron the finished doily. Check the temperature of the iron on a

Fig. 4–25 Embroidered net doily.

scrap of net to avoid scorching. The finished piece can be used as a doily or displayed in a frame.

Pattern explanations

All dotted areas are filled with running stitch in one strand of embroidery floss.

Round berries on stems can be outlined, outlined and filled with running stitch, or made into round eyelets.

121

Fig. 4–26 One-half of the floral net embroidery pattern for the doily.

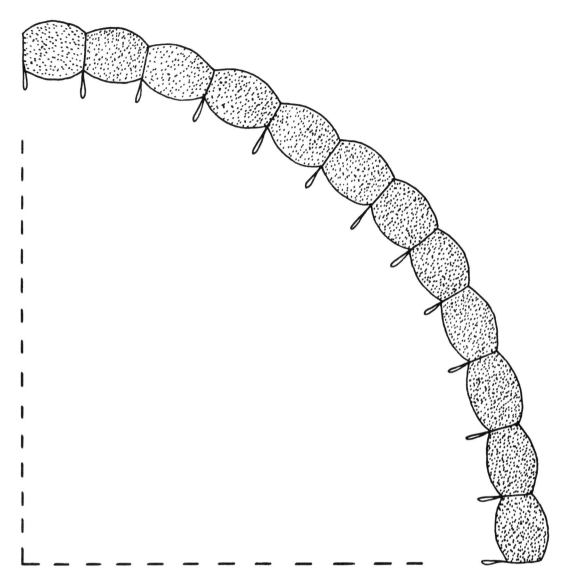

Fig. 4–27 One-quarter of the scallop design for the net doily.

CHAPTER

5

Eyelet Embroidery and Cutwork

COMBINING STITCHERY
WITH OPENWORK TEXTURES

Always in search of new techniques, needleworkers, not content with just embellishing the surface of their fabric with a variety of stitches in cotton, silk, wool, or precious metals, began to change the background itself by cutting or punching holes of different sizes and shapes. This was how *broderie anglaise*, also known as eyelet embroidery, was born. Although some of the oldest examples can be found on samplers dating back to the end of the 17th century, eyelet embroidery did not become fashionable until the middle of the 18th century. In the 19th century, Victorian women found innumerable uses for eyelet patterns, which they used on baby clothes, house linens, petticoats, chemises, camisoles, long drawers, nightdresses, and on the flounces of dresses. The demand for eyelet embroidery became so great that a sizable cottage industry grew up, especially in Scotland and Ireland.

In eyelet embroidery, small "eyelet" holes are cut with scissors or made by a stiletto to form a pattern or motif. The cut holes can be round, oval, or triangular, while eyelets made with a stiletto are always round. Interestingly enough, 18th-century eyelet designs employed no embroidery stitches, apart from a running stitch to strengthen the edges and the overcast stitch. Every element of a design, even the leaves and stems of flowers, was constructed of eyelets. Eventually, to embellish the patterns even more, small motifs were embroidered in padded satin stitch and stem stitch, and scalloped borders covered with close buttonhole stitch were added.

Eyelet patterns, both geometric and floral, were transferred onto white or natural cambric, a closely woven linen or cotton fabric similar to

Fig. 5–1 Detail from a tablecloth embroidered in satin and stem stitch with eyelets.

muslin or batiste. The embroidery was done in strong white thread. The embroideress needed a good needle and sharp scissors and a stiletto for making eyelets. The work was usually held in hand, not placed on a frame or in a hoop. The embroidery was durable enough to survive frequent washings.

Eyelets were also used in other techniques, such as Ayrshire work, sometimes also called "flowering," which developed simultaneously with eyelet embroidery and combined eyelets with drawn thread work and lace filling stitches.

POLISH FOLK EYELET EMBROIDERY

Eyelet embroidery became fashionable in the Polish countryside in the 18th century, if not earlier. One variety popular in southeastern Poland around Lancut is probably older, and combines round eyelets with geometrical patterns embroidered in satin stitch based on counting background threads (Fig. 5–2). These designs resemble motifs from late Re-

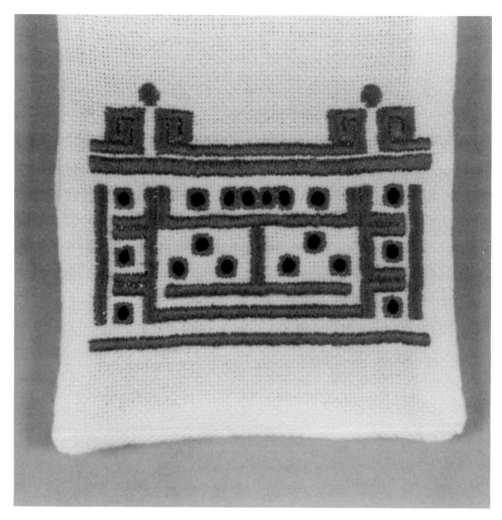

Fig. 5–2 An old Polish geometrical eyelet design in red floss.

naissance pottery and architectural details found on the facades of Renaissance buildings.

Typical eyelet embroidery was probably copied by villagers in Poland from city fashions or by village women who were employed in Polish manor homes. Of course, we can only speculate that country women on their market trips to town admired the embroideries worn by the burgher wives and then copied the clothing at home. Then again, maybe some of the village girls were sent to towns to work as maids or to learn a craft and upon returning home introduced new fashions to their friends and neighbors. Ladies from the manor homes may have commissioned the more talented needlewomen from the villages and introduced them to the fashionable techniques and patterns that were circulating throughout Europe in French, German, and English fashion magazines.

Whichever road it took to reach the Polish villages, eyelet embroidery found its place in decorating costumes and household items and achieved a high level of technical execution and beauty of design. The most vigorous period in its development came in the late 19th century during a time of relative prosperity, when farmers had more money to spend and more time to think about their clothing. The most beautiful eyelet embroidery was created throughout southern Poland and especially in the area called "Little Poland." At that time in many areas of southern Poland all the sewing and embroidery was still done by hand, as sewing machines were introduced only in the 1920s.

Most eyelet designs were done on white fabric, but around Sieradz, beautiful patterns were embroidered on pink-and-white striped cloth.

During the 18th and much of the 19th centuries, the sewing needs of the household were taken care of by the wife with the help of her older daughters. But when the fashion in clothing introduced more intricate designs, a group of village specialists emerged. These were talented women who were forced by circumstances to seek additional means of employment. Some prudent mothers tried to secure their daughters' future by providing them with a needlework education. For example, in the Podhale region, girls of fourteen and fifteen were trained in embroidery by a skilled embroideress who either charged a fee for teaching or assigned household chores to her students. The girls had to supply their own fabric and thread and usually started by making a sampler of stitches and motifs. After they achieved a certain level of proficiency, the girls embroidered garments for themselves and designed their own patterns. When machine embroidery became popular, after learning handwork, the girls would be taught the basics of machine embroidery, which they would spend long hours practicing on their own.

Most eyelet embroidery was done on commission. Wealthy women often commissioned eyelet embroidery for their daughters' trousseaus. The client would visit the needleworker's house to select patterns. Most commissions were completed during the winter months, when outside chores were fewer.

The embroideress needed only a few tools, such as a needle, a stiletto, sometimes a hoop, and a pencil. She would start by drawing semicircles along the edge for scallops, using pots or dishes as patterns or even coins for tiny scallops. After the scallop outlines were drawn, the patterns were fitted inside them. Often they were drawn freehand or copied through carbon paper. She would then cover the outlines with running stitch and complete the eyelets with overcast stitch, stem stitch, drawn thread work, and filling stitches such as the overcast wheel stitch. Many of the open spaces were decorated with a variety of filling stitches, but in the 19th century, the work was simplified and the designs were mainly based on round and oval eyelets and elements of drawn-thread work. In some regions, to simulate filling stitches, needleworkers covered larger cut-out areas with embroidered tulle.

The use of a hoop in handwork depended on the personal preference of the embroideress, while machine work required it. Machine eyelet embroidery is done through only one layer of cloth, and the round eyelets, instead of being punched through with a stiletto, are cut with scissors and hemmed by machine. Machine-made embroidery usually has larger openings than eyelets done by hand.

Eyelet embroidery decorated men's outfits as well as women's, especially on collars, shirt fronts, and cuffs. On special occasions, men wore heavily starched eyelet-embroidered shirts, and in southern Poland, around Podhale, women often wore two shirts with their holiday outfits. The bottom shirt had short, tight-fitting embroidered sleeves, and the top shirt, more of a blouse, had elaborate patterns decorating a large, round collar, cuffs, and long sleeves (Fig. 5–3). As fashions changed, some women also embroidered shirt fronts to display even more needlework from beneath their low-cut bodices. In southeastern Poland, near Dabrowa Tarnowska, instead of wearing a bodice over an embroidered shirt, women occasionally wore eyelet blouses resembling short jackets. Near Pszczyna, short, wide shirt sleeves on blouses and nightgowns were gathered in the middle with a ribbon pulled through a row of round eyelets to create balloon sleeves.

In less prosperous villages, women who could not afford richly embroidered shirts wore eyelet collars. For reasons of economy, the collars were often detachable and could be worn with several different blouses. Older women, particularly widows, wore detachable collars with modest patterns. But the more prosperous, fashionable women were not content with only eyelet blouses or collars. They also had long bloomers and petticoats

128

Fig. 5-3 Woman's holiday shirt from Podhale embroidered by machine on white cotton.

edged with scallops and eyelet patterns. In Podhale, white embroidered petticoats (Fig. 5–4) became part of holiday outfits. Around Dabrowa Tarnowska, women wore embroidered petticoats on top of another petticoat in a solid color to accent the eyelets and drawn-thread motifs. Some

Fig. 5–4 A modestly decorated petticoat from Podhale embroidered by machine on white cotton.

petticoats, embroidered on linen, were so beautiful that they were worn without the top skirt.

Aprons also became fashionable as a decorative accessory. They were often given as bridal presents or presented to a girl by a young man as a token of his affection and a sign of betrothal. Some aprons had alternating strips of eyelet and crocheted lace.

Fig. 5–5 Woman's holiday apron embroidered by machine on white cotton.

Eyelet embroidery became such a favorite that it was also found on long white shawls and on the bonnets and headscarves worn by married women. Many of the old shawls have survived thanks to the custom of presenting the most beautiful pieces to the church to serve as altar cloths and towels used during Mass.

Babies were christened in embroidered outfits and slept under embroidered coverlets. Mountain cottages had embroidered curtains in the windows, shelves were covered with embroidered doilies, and the bed was stacked high with huge feather pillows in exquisitely embroidered white pillowcases. White embroidered sheets were often used as bedspreads. To display other pieces of eyelet embroidery, women would hang huge pillows over a long, horizontal bar near the ceiling. When an eyelet garment went out of fashion, the women would recycle it, perhaps making a set of curtains out of an apron or a christening gown out of a petticoat.

Until the late 19th century eyelet patterns were geometrical. Scalloped edges became an integral part of each design, and, depending on the region, were either shallow, rounded, or finished with sharp points. Large, rounded scallops were often decorated with smaller ones. Scalloped edges were secured with a buttonhole or overcast stitch or, for an additional decorative effect, with a row or two of round eyelets. The designs that extended beyond the scallops were filled with eyelets arranged to form circles, stars, squares, or hearts for a geometrical pattern, or with roses, thistles, edelweiss, or grapevine for a floral design. Newer embroideries from the Podhale region, especially machine embroideries, were made with round and oval eyelets to create different shapes, while the older designs and all those done by hand were created by combining eyelets with embroidery in flat stitches, which is less lacy but more varied artistically.

In most of the older garments, the placement of the design is connected with the structure of the item, for example, horizontal strips of design on an apron. The newer garments show the departure from the connection between the pattern and the structure. So the sleeves of a blouse, instead of rows of designs, show large compositions spreading to each side.

EYELET EMBROIDERY TECHNIQUE

Every motif in eyelet embroidery is outlined in running stitch. A stiletto is used to pierce small, round eyelets (Fig. 5–6), and after the eyelet is opened, the edges are strengthened with an overcast stitch to cover the edge of the hole as well as the row of running stitch.

132

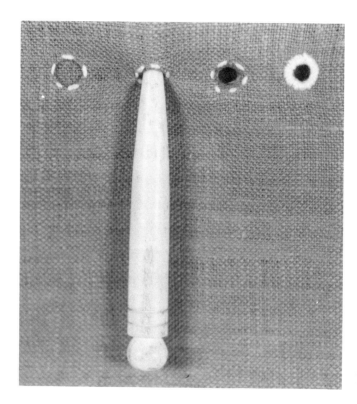

Fig. 5–6 Sequence of steps in punching out and overcasting small round eyelets.

When making large round, oval or tear-shaped eyelets, the eyelets must be cut with very sharp scissors instead of with a stiletto. The cutting is done after the outlines of the design are covered with running stitch, as in the case of small eyelets. When cutting a motif with scissors, care has to be taken not to cut out fabric along the line of the drawing. A slit has to be made through the middle of the eyelet (Fig. 5–7). Then the edges of the slit are folded to the wrong side and secured with overcast stitch. If bits of fabric remain after completing the stitching, they have to be trimmed carefully so that the stitching will not be damaged.

Eyelets should be made one at a time to prevent distortions in the design. Larger round eyelets can be decorated with a filling motif, while drawn-thread work can be employed inside elements with irregular outlines.

For a scalloped piece, the scallops should be drawn ½" or 1" from the edge of the fabric, strengthened with running stitch (Fig. 5–9), then cov-

133

Fig. 5–7 The fabric in a tear-shaped eyelet is slit and the corners tacked on the wrong side.

ered with overcast or buttonhole stitch (Fig. 5–10). The excess fabric is then cut off very close to the stitching (Fig. 5–11).

CUTWORK TECHNIQUE

Cutwork is similar to eyelet embroidery in that the surface of the fabric is decorated by cutting away parts of it to achieve a light, lacy effect. In eyelet embroidery, the holes themselves form the design and the background is left untouched. In the most famous cutwork techniques—Renaissance embroidery (sometimes called Guipure) and Richelieu work—the background of each motif is cut out. Because of the amount of open space in these two techniques, bars are formed to strengthen the pattern and hold the elements together. Richelieu work, named after the French

Fig. 5–8 Slitting a large round eyelet.

134

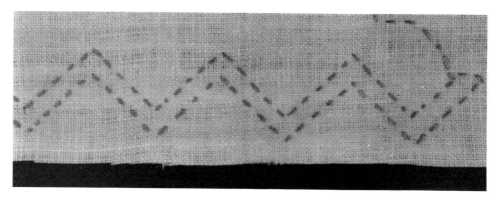

Fig. 5–9 Scallops should be drawn an inch or two from the edge of the fabric and then outlined in running stitch. If the buttonhole stitch is to be wide, outline the scallops with two rows of running stitch.

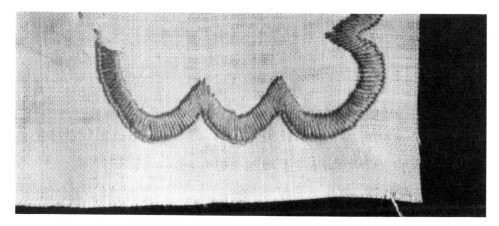

Fig. 5–10 Scallops are covered with buttonhole stitch, the looped edge on the outside.

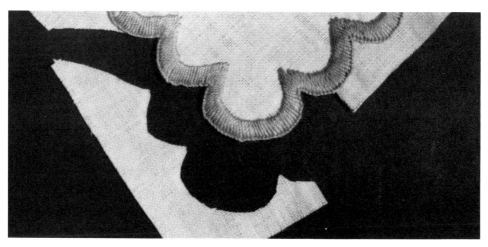

Fig. 5–11 Excess fabric is cut off very close to the looped stitches.

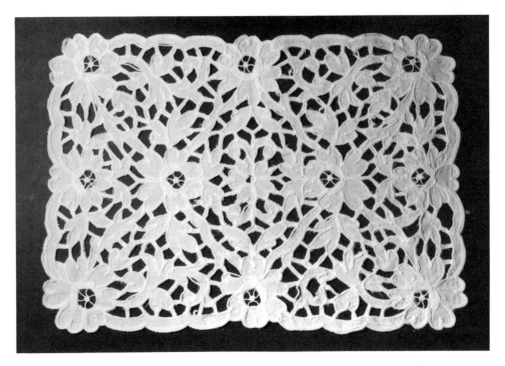

Fig. 5–12 A cutwork piece executed with a crochet hook (tambour work). The edges are strengthened with chain stitch.

cardinal Richelieu (1585–1642), who wore embellished cutwork garments, is more open than Renaissance embroidery and its bars are decorated with loops, or picots. Renaissance and Richelieu work decorated white collars, cuffs, and edgings in floral designs.

The difference between eyelet embroidery and Richelieu and Renaissance work is evident in the work method. While eyelets are cut out or punched out and then overcast, here the cutting is done *after* all the stitching is completed. First, the outlines are covered with running stitch and the bars are formed. The foundation for the bars is made by spanning the space to be cut out with three or four threads, then strengthening it with a buttonhole stitch and, in Richelieu work, adding the picots. The buttonhole stitch is used to cover all the outlines along with the running stitch. The looped edge of the stitch always faces the side of the pattern which is to be cut out. After all the stitching is completed, fabric is trimmed around the looped edges and under the bars.

136

Fig. 5–13 A cutwork doily executed in buttonhole bars and small round eyelets.

Richelieu and Renaissance work is done on white linen or cotton in either white linen or cotton thread such as pearl cotton or cotton embroidery floss. Colored thread was popular in folk embroidery. In southern Poland, women's white holiday aprons were edged on three sides with flowers, mostly roses, embroidered in the Renaissance technique in red thread. Around Lowicz, in central Poland, blouse sleeves were edged with a wide floral scroll, embroidered in white. The appearance of Renaissance work in Polish folk costume is a relatively new phenomenon and probably originated only at the beginning of the 20th century.

Pillowcase
(Color plate 15 and Fig. 5–14)

Materials

Cotton pillowcase in any color
White embroidery floss (1 skein)
Stiletto
Needles
Embroidery hoop
Transfer tools

Instructions

The pattern in Figure 5–15 represents one-half of the design. To complete the design, add another identical half so that point "a" matches point "b". Transfer the pattern to the pillowcase. (I placed the design vertically, approximately 4″ from the opening of the case.)

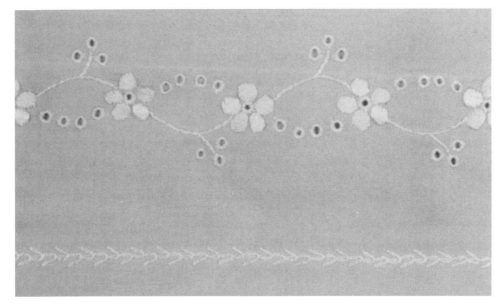

Fig. 5–14 Eyelet-edged pillowcase.

138

Fig. 5–15 One-half of the embroidery pattern for the eyelet pillowcase.

Punch out the tiny round eyelets with a stiletto and cover the edges with overcast stitch. Use stem stitch for all the stems and satin stitch for the petals of the flowers. All stitching is done in two strands of embroidery floss. Cover the machine stitching on the case opening with feather stitch in two strands of floss.

Wash and iron the finished pillowcase.

Pattern explanations

Solid circles represent small round eyelets.
Outlined petals are embroidered in satin stitch.
All curving lines are embroidered in stem stitch.

Toddler Overalls
(Color plate 17 and Fig. 5–16)

Finished size: approximately 17″ long

Materials
Blue cotton fabric (approximately 26″ by 34″)
White cotton fabric (approximately 29″ by 34″)
Red sewing thread; white sewing thread
Two red buttons
Red embroidery floss (1 skein)
Needles
Stiletto
Embroidery hoop
Transfer tools and materials for enlarging the design
Red bias tape (optional)

Instructions
Note: Seam allowances are not included in the patterns.

To enlarge the pattern for the overalls (Fig. 5–17), prepare a grid with 1½″ squares. Copy the pattern square by square to the large grid. Make the pattern for the overalls and the pocket. Add the seam allowances and cut out the pattern on the fold from the blue and the white fabric. Do the same with the pocket pattern. Transfer the eyelet embroidery patterns to the blue fabric for the overalls (Fig. 5–18) and pocket (Fig. 5–19), following the pattern in Figure 5–20.

Complete the eyelet designs, embroidering the outlines with stem stitch. Punch out the blackened circles for the round eyelets with a stiletto and overcast. All the stitching is done in three strands of red floss.

After completing the stitching, assemble the overalls and sew on the pocket. Make two buttonholes in the front straps and sew on two buttons to

Fig. 5–16 Eyelet-
trimmed toddler
overalls.

the back straps (which, when buttoned, cross at the back). If you wish, outline the overalls with red bias tape.

Pattern explanations

All solid circles represent eyelets.
All the outlines are embroidered in stem stitch.

141

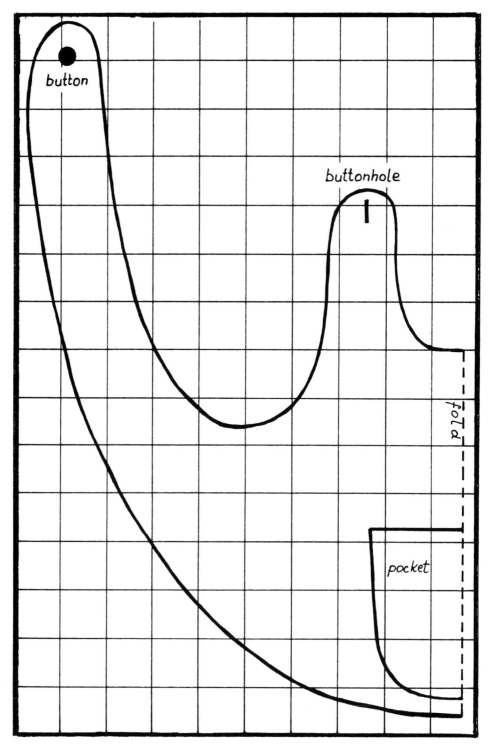

Fig. 5–17 Pattern for the toddler overalls.

Fig. 5–18 Motif a for the overalls.

Fig. 5–19 Motif b for the pocket of the overalls.

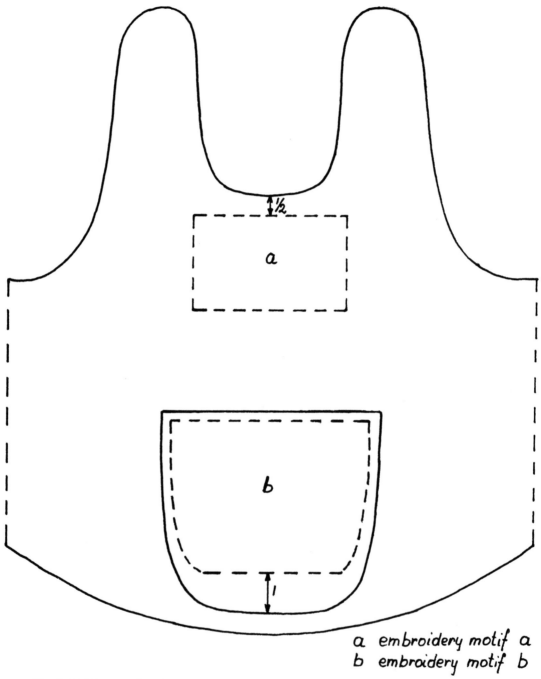

a   embroidery motif a
b   embroidery motif b

Fig. 5–20 Diagram for placing motifs on the toddler overalls (see Figs. 5–18 and 5–19).

144

Square Eyelet Tablecloth

(Figs. 5–21 and 5–22)

Finished size: 53″ by 53″

Materials

56″ by 56″ square of cream-colored linen
White sewing thread
White embroidery floss
White pearl cotton No. 8
Embroidery hoop
Stiletto
Needles
Transfer tools

Instructions

Note: The pattern in Figure 5–23 does not include hem allowances.

Make sure that the piece of linen is perfectly square. Then, 2½″ from each edge, pull enough threads to form a $^3/_{16}$″-wide strip. Make sure that the drawn threads match at each corner. (See Chapter 7 on drawn-thread techniques.)

Hem the square so that the distance between the drawn-thread strip and the edge of the tablecloth equals 1″. Miter the corners and finish the drawn-thread strip with ladder hemstitch in two strands of white embroidery floss. After hemming the square, begin the eyelet embroidery. First, draw and transfer all the motifs (Figs 5–24 through 5–27), following the pattern in Figure 5–23. Pattern "a" in Figure 5–24 gives only one-half of the design. The second half is a mirror image of the first half. (*Note:* It is not necessary to make the drawing of the whole tablecloth. Each motif can be transferred separately, but be careful to space them correctly.)

With two strands of floss, outline all the solid areas in the drawings with running stitch. Punch out the solid circles with a stiletto and overcast with one strand of pearl cotton. All the solid tear-shaped motifs are to be slit in the middle and the raw edges turned to the wrong side, then overcast with one strand of pearl cotton. Fill all the outlined areas with satin

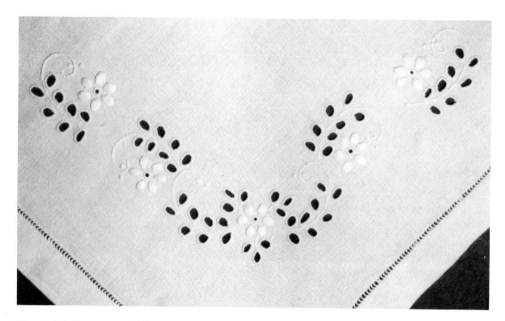

Fig. 5–21 Corner motif for the square eyelet tablecloth.

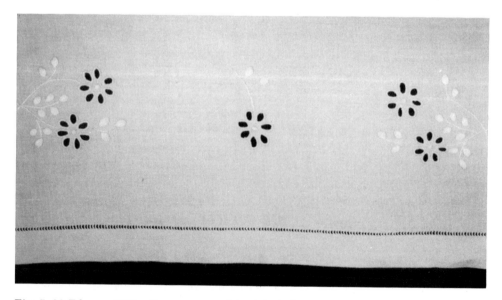

Fig. 5–22 Edge motif for the square eyelet tablecloth.

146

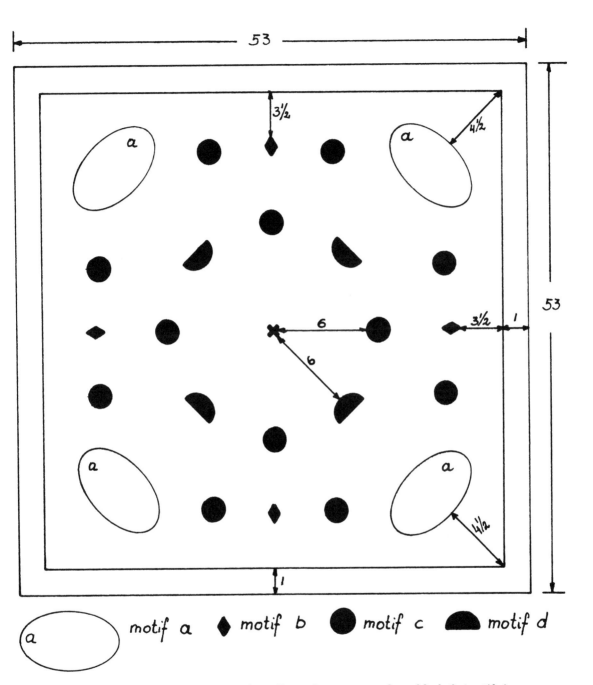

Fig. 5–23 Diagram for placement of motifs on the square eyelet tablecloth (motifs in Figs. 5–24 through 5–27).

Fig. 5–24 One-half of motif a.

148

stitch and cover all the stems with stem stitch in one strand of pearl cotton. Wash, lightly starch, and iron the tablecloth.

Pattern explanations

All solid circles represent eyelets.
All open areas are filled with satin stitch.
All curving lines are embroidered in stem stitch.

Fig. 5–25 Motif b.

Fig. 5–26 Motif c.

Fig. 5-27 Motif d.

Cutwork Collar

(Color plate 11, Figs. 5–28 and 5–29)

Materials

15″ by 18″ rectangle of white cotton fabric
White embroidery floss
White sewing thread
Needles
Embroidery hoop
White bias tape (½″ wide)
Transfer tools

Instructions

Complete the drawing for the whole collar, matching the broken lines along 1–2 in Figures 5–30 and 5–31. Transfer the pattern to the fabric, but do not cut it out!

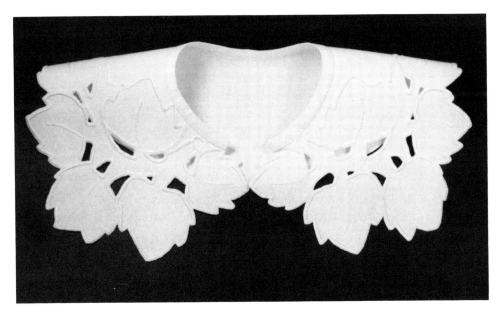

Fig. 5–28 Cutwork collar.

Fig. 5–29 Detail of the front of the cutwork collar.

With two strands of embroidery floss, cover all the double lines on the leaf pattern with chain stitch. Outline the rest of the design and the outer edge of the collar with running stitch in two strands of floss. Cover the running-stitch outlines with buttonhole stitch, remembering that the looped edge should face the outside of the design. (The inner edge of the collar, where the collar will be the closest to the neck, is not embroidered.) Cover both front corners of the collar and the outer edge with buttonhole stitch. Now cut out the collar. Cut out all the solid areas between the leaves.

Note: The second line on the drawing, placed ¼″ from the neckline opening, marks the stitching line of the bias tape. Finish the neckline with bias tape.

Wash, lightly starch, and iron the collar.

Pattern explanations

Double lines are embroidered in chain stitch.
Solid areas are cut out.

Fig. 5–30 Cutwork
collar pattern a.

bias tape

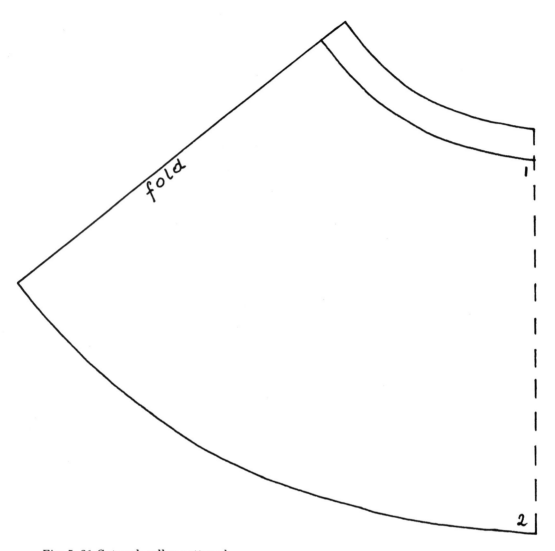

Fig. 5–31 Cutwork collar pattern b.

154

Doily with Pansies
(Fig. 5–32)

Finished size: approximately 8″ by 8″

Materials
10″ by 10″ square of white cotton fabric
White embroidery floss
Needles
Stiletto
Embroidery hoop
Transfer tools

Instructions

The pattern in Figure 5–33 represents one-quarter of the design. Complete the drawing of the entire design and transfer it to the fabric. With two strands of floss, cover all the outlines marked with double lines in running stitch.

Place the fabric in a hoop. Complete the buttonhole bars, which are marked with straight, heavy lines joining the flowers to the inner circle of the doily. With a stiletto, punch out the dotted circles and cover the edges with buttonhole stitch. Go over all the outlines with buttonhole stitch. (*Note:* The looping edge of the buttonhole stitch always faces the outside of the motifs.) Embroider the short single lines inside the flowers with stem stitch.

After completing the stitching, wash and iron the piece and carefully trim the excess fabric around the flowers and underneath the bars. Cut close to the buttonhole stitching, but be careful not to damage the stitching.

Wash, lightly starch, and iron the doily again.

Pattern explanations

Double lines are embroidered in buttonhole stitch.
Dotted circles are round eyelets.
Straight heavy lines are buttonhole bars.
Short lines inside the petals are embroidered with stem stitch.

Fig. 5–32 Doily with pansies.

Fig. 5–33 One-quarter of the pattern for the doily with pansies.

Summer Skirt
(Fig. 5–34)

Materials

Any summer skirt in plain cotton in a simple design gathered at waist (the
 fabric for the skirt shown in Figure 5–34 is heavy unbleached muslin)
Coffee-colored pearl cotton No. 8
Off-white sewing thread
Needles
Embroidery hoop
Transfer tools

Instructions for cutwork strip

The pattern in Figure 5–35 represents only a section of the design,
which consists of two repeated elements—the rose and the leaves. To complete the design of any length, the section between points "a" and "b" has
to be repeated.

Draw the design and transfer it onto the skirt. The design on the skirt
is placed 7″ from the bottom edge, but the placement depends on the length
of the entire skirt.

Fig. 5–34 Cutwork strip from the summer skirt.

Fig. 5–35 Section of
the cutwork design
for the summer
skirt.

Cover all the double-line outlines with running stitch in off-white thread. Then, complete the buttonhole bars. (The buttonhole bars are indicated by heavy solid lines.) Next, cover all the double lines with buttonhole stitch, keeping in mind that the looped edge should always face the outside of the motifs. And finally, embroider all the single curving lines inside the flowers and leaves in stem stitch. All stitching is done in one strand of pearl cotton.

Wash and iron the finished skirt and trim the excess fabric from under the bars, cutting very close to the buttonhole stitch.

Pattern explanations

Double lines are covered with buttonhole stitch.
Heavy solid lines represent buttonhole bars.
Single lines are embroidered in stem stitch.

Snutki

ORIGINS OF SPIDERWEB EMBROIDERY

The Polish origins of spiderweb embroidery, an unusual form of cut-work, probably go back to old Italian laces, which were so admired by village women that they copied the designs for their own use, ingeniously adapting the intricate lace-making technique to embroidery.

Spiderweb embroidery, known in Poland as "Snutki," became especially popular in "Great Poland," around Poznan, and women decorated bonnets, round collars, sleeves (between the cuff and the elbow), and aprons of their folk costumes with it.

In the 19th century, when clothing decorated with tulle embroidery became fashionable, spiderweb work was used for household items, such as pillowcases and table linens, and linens for the church and manor homes.

Spiderweb embroidery was usually done by the young unmarried women in the villages or by the poor women who supplemented their incomes by accepting commissions from the wealthy women of the manor homes. Large pieces such as altar cloths were divided into sections and were worked on by several women and offered to local churches in the hope that they might receive a special blessing for their pious labor, such as the return of their husbands from war.

Spiderweb embroidery was always done in white cotton thread on a white background of linen or cotton. Apart from a needle and a pair of sharp scissors, the only other tool needed was a bone stiletto to make eyelets. The design was worked out on paper and then transferred to the fabric. The women did not have compasses, so they used pots, plates, and drinking glasses to make perfectly round circles. To make templates of other shapes such as stars, they folded and cut paper, while flowers were drawn from nature.

After transferring the design, all the outlines were covered with running stitch to strengthen the edges and to add a raised or relief effect. For an even higher relief, chain stitch was used instead of running stitch. The spiderwebs were created by connecting motifs with thread anchored on the inside of each motif but close to the running-stitch outline (see Fig. 6–1).

The next step was to complete the edgings and eyelet embroidery. All the outlines were covered with buttonhole or overcast stitches and the eyelets pierced with a stiletto and overcast. After the stitching was completed, the piece was washed and carefully ironed on the wrong side to avoid scorching the design. Only then was it time for the most delicate part of the work — cutting out the fabric between the stitched motifs. First, a slit was made in the fabric between the spiderwebs. The cutting was done on the wrong side but close to the stitched edges. At this stage it was easy even for an experienced embroideress to accidentally cut one of the spider-

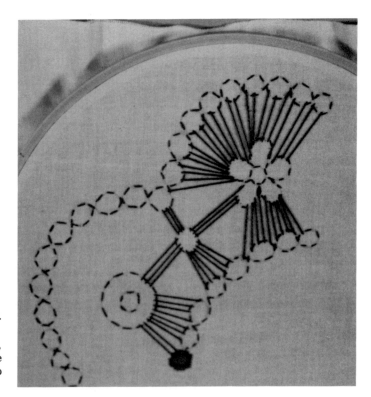

Fig. 6–1 Spiderwebs are created by connecting the motifs with long threads. After the stitching and eyelets are completed, the fabric beneath the threads is cut away to create a lacy effect.

162

web threads. If this happened, the cut thread had to be immediately fastened by a stitch or two to avoid the "domino effect" of unraveling all the other threads. After the fabric was cut out, the piece was washed, starched, blocked, and ironed.

Large Doily
(Color plate 10 and Fig. 6–2)

Finished size: approximately 11½" in diameter

Materials
15" by 15" square of white cotton fabric
White 3-cord crochet cotton, size 30
White sewing thread
Stiletto
Needles
Embroidery hoop
Transfer tools

Instructions
The pattern in Figure 6–3 represents one-quarter of the whole design. Complete the drawing of the entire design and transfer it to fabric. (*Note:* The thin straight lines signifying laid threads do not have to be transferred.) With white sewing thread, outline the whole design in running stitch. Place the piece in a hoop and connect all the motifs with straight lines of crochet cotton (see Fig. 6–3). Anchor the threads close to the running stitch but always on the inside of the motif. Make sure that you keep an even tension on the thread to keep the fabric from puckering.

Complete all the round eyelets by punching them out with a stiletto or slitting with scissors and covering the raw edges with buttonhole stitch. Complete all the outlines marked with heavy black lines, also in buttonhole stitch. After completing the stitching, take the fabric off the hoop and wash and iron it. Cut off all extra fabric underneath the laid threads. Make the cuts close to the stitched edges. Wash, starch, and iron the doily.

Fig. 6–2 Large spiderweb doily.

Pattern explanations

Heavy black outlines are embroidered in buttonhole stitch.

Thin straight lines represent laid thread.

Dotted areas represent fabric.

All the stitching (the buttonhole stitch and the long stitches forming laid threads) is done in one strand of crochet cotton.

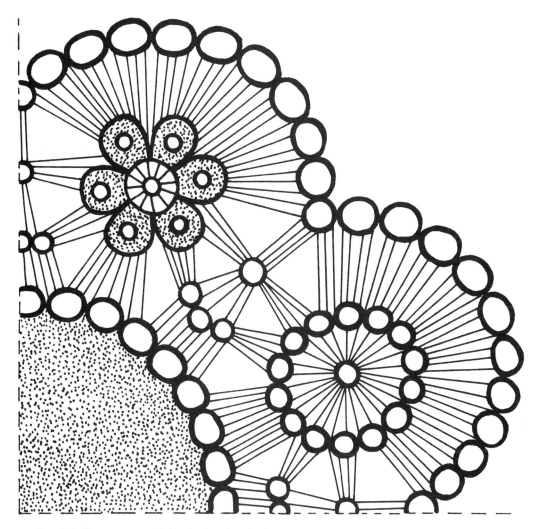

Fig. 6–3 One-quarter of the design for the large spiderweb doily.

Small Doily
(Fig. 6–4)

Finished size: approximately 9½″ in diameter

Materials

12″ by 12″ square of white cotton fabric
White 3-cord crochet cotton, size 30
White sewing thread
Stiletto
Needles
Embroidery hoop
Transfer tools

Instructions

The pattern in Figure 6–5 represents one-quarter of the design. Complete the drawing of the entire design and transfer it to the fabric. (*Note:* The thin straight lines signifying laid threads do not have to be transferred.) With white sewing thread, outline the whole design in running stitch. Place the piece in a hoop and connect all the motifs with straight lines of crochet cotton (see Fig. 6–5). Anchor the threads close to the running stitch but always on the inside of the motif. Make sure that you keep an even tension on the thread to keep the fabric from puckering.

Complete all the round eyelets by punching them out with a stiletto or slitting with scissors and covering the raw edges with buttonhole stitch. Complete all the outlines marked with heavy black lines, also in buttonhole stitch. After completing the stitching, take the fabric off the hoop and wash and iron it. Cut off all extra fabric underneath the laid threads. Make the cuts close to the stitched edges.

Wash, starch, and iron the doily.

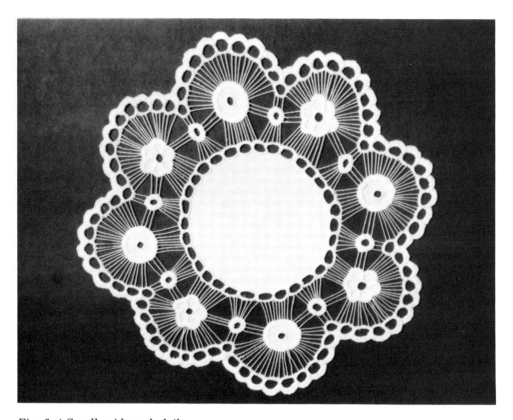

Fig. 6–4 Small spiderweb doily.

Pattern explanations

Heavy black outlines are embroidered in buttonhole stitch.

Thin straight lines represent laid thread.

Dotted areas represent fabric.

All the stitching (the buttonhole stitch and the long stitches forming laid threads) is done in one strand of crochet cotton.

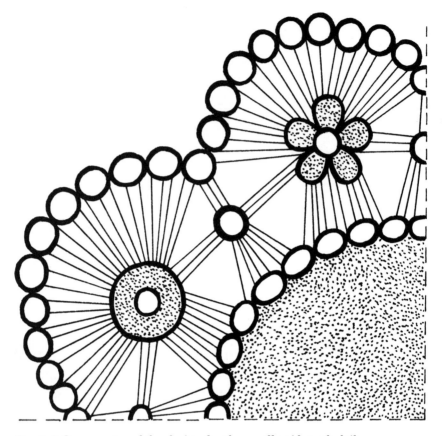

Fig. 6–5 One-quarter of the design for the small spiderweb doily.

Round Lace Doily
(Fig. 6–6)

Finished size: approximately 10½″ in diameter

Materials

13″ by 13″ square of white cotton fabric
White 3-cord crochet cotton, size 30
White sewing thread
Stiletto
Needles
Embroidery hoop
Transfer tools

Instructions

The pattern in Figure 6-7 represents one-quarter of the design. Complete the drawing of the entire design and transfer it to the fabric. (*Note:* The thin straight lines signifying laid threads do not have to be transferred.) With white sewing thread, outline the whole design in running stitch. Place the piece in a hoop and connect all the motifs with straight lines of crochet cotton (see Fig. 6–7). Anchor the threads close to the running stitch but always on the inside of the motif. Make sure that you keep an even tension on the thread to keep the fabric from puckering.

Complete all the round and oval eyelets by punching them out with a stiletto or slitting with scissors and covering the raw edges with buttonhole stitch. Complete all the outlines marked with heavy black lines, also in buttonhole stitch. After completing the stitching, take the fabric off the hoop and wash and iron it. Cut off all extra fabric underneath the laid threads. Make the cuts close to the stitched edges.

Wash, starch, and iron the doily.

Pattern explanations

Heavy black outlines are embroidered in buttonhole stitch.
Thin straight lines represent laid thread.
Dotted areas represent fabric.
All the stitching (the buttonhole stitch and the long stitches forming laid threads) is done in one strand of crochet cotton.

169

Fig. 6–6 Round lace doily.

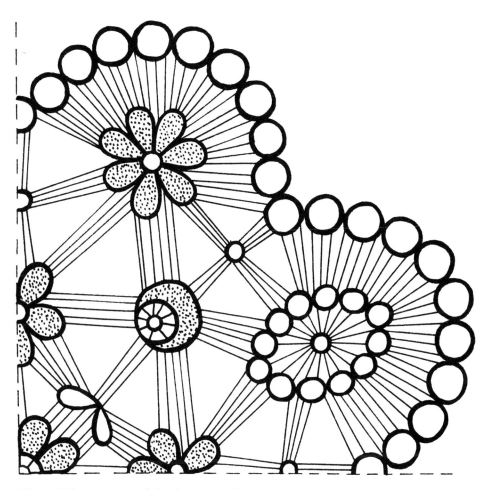

Fig. 6–7 One-quarter of the design for the round lace doily.

7

Drawn Thread Work

A FINE, OLD NEEDLEWORK TECHNIQUE

Drawn thread work is one of the oldest of needlework techniques and is the predecessor of most laces. The ancient Egyptians used the technique on their exquisite linen cloth, and since then drawn thread work has always been associated with the finest linen. The stitching was done with a matching thread, often with "ravelings"—the threads pulled out of the warp or weft of the fabric. Ravelings were used for two reasons—to have the thread match the background fabric and to make use of the threads withdrawn from the fabric.

Drawn thread work is sometimes confused with drawn fabric work because of the similarity in terms, but the two techniques are distinctly different. In drawn thread work, the structure of the fabric is changed as the threads are drawn from the warp and weft of the fabric itself and are used for the actual stitching. In drawn fabric work, also called pulled work, the background threads of the fabric are pulled in opposite directions and bunched to create a series of tiny openings arranged into a lacy pattern.

Through the centuries, many varieties of drawn thread work evolved. For example, Egyptian and Coptic embroideries were executed in a needleweaving technique where the design was woven over the warp of the fabric after the weft was removed, or vice versa. Needleweaving has also been popular in northern Asia and around the Mediterranean, where beautiful examples can be found, as in Turkish folk costumes.

Another form of drawn thread work emerged in the Middle Ages. In 13th-century Germany, drawn thread work, called *opus teutonicum*, was made in convents. The pieces best known for the artistry of the design and the perfection of the execution were altar cloths and Lenten veils, which screened the altar and the choir from worshipers during Lent. The embroidery on the Lenten veils depicted figures of saints and scenes from the Old and New Testaments. The figures were embroidered on white linen with a variety of stitches executed in linen thread, while the background was mesh-like, an effect created by withdrawing threads in regular intervals from both the warp and the weft of the fabric.

The Renaissance shifted the interest of needleworkers from creating masterpieces mainly for the church to decorating secular clothing. Numerous pattern books printed in 16th-century Italy provided Europeans with innovative ideas for decorating their clothing. Indeed, at that time, drawn thread work was considered an integral part of sewing. Garments or lengths of linen cloth were hemmed in an ornamental hemstitch. Cloth was woven on narrow looms, and several widths had to be sewn together to make even simple garments, so the seams were also decorated with hemstitching. Drawn thread work also decorated wristbands, necklines, and the front openings of shirts. Elizabethan women favored coifs covered with drawn thread work, which not only were beautiful but proved to be cool on hot summer days. Drawn thread work was also placed along the hem and on both sides of each seam of men's shirts.

During the 16th century, the fashion for drawn thread work moved into the countryside. In Scandinavia, it became slowly transformed into the Hardanger work of Norway and the Hedebo work of Denmark. These techniques were used to decorate shirts, underclothing, pillowcases and sheets, headcloths, and curtains. Hedebo work flourished in the 18th century, when the first designs were copied from woodcarvings and carved furniture. In Hedebo work, threads were withdrawn from the background of the linen fabric and the remaining threads were stitched over to create a mesh. Hardanger work was also done on linen, but a geometrical design was embroidered first, then threads cut and withdrawn from the fabric to create open spaces, which were then filled with stitching.

During the 17th and 18th centuries, drawn thread work continued to play an important role in domestic needlework and in women's fashion. It embellished stomachers with delicate designs as well as aprons, which became popular among aristocratic ladies in the 18th century. Aprons were embroidered in a combination of darning, buttonhole stitching, and drawn thread work with compositions of birds and flowers. Drawn thread work became so popular that it was included in the needlework education of every young girl, who learned different needlework techniques by making samplers. Considered to be one of the more difficult techniques, drawn thread work was included only in the student's second sampler, while the first one was devoted to stitches in colored threads. It has to be remembered, however, that the girls working on these samplers were only eight or nine years old. The samplers were made on white or yellow linen and combined drawn thread work, cutwork, and Reticella lace. Needleweaving was also included in 18th-century American samplers, and in the Pennsylvania German community women made towels in the form of a sampler and decorated them with drawn thread and cross-stitched alphabets and names.

Other variants of drawn thread work are Russian drawn-ground work, which resembles *opus teutonicum*, and Levkara work, or Cyprus embroidery, which is characterized by geometrical designs and wide fringes created by withdrawing threads from the fabric. The drawn thread technique is also used in Ayrshire work and in some forms of Tenerife lace and Persian openwork.

POLISH FOLK DRAWN THREAD WORK

In Poland, drawn thread work has always been popular among country folk. It reached its highest level of development in southern Poland, where many garments were made out of homespun and woven linen. Some claim that drawn thread work originated among the shepherds in Podhale, who used it to finish the edges of a garment in order to prevent the fabric from raveling. Until the late 1920s, drawn thread work was used on men's clothing, especially on undergarments. The bottom of summer pants and underpants sewn out of linen was finished with a row of drawn thread and then a section of fabric unraveled to form a small fringe. In the Spisz area, drawn thread work edged shirt bottoms and sleeves. The sleeves were usually decorated with wider designs and often included needleweaving. It is safe to say that drawn thread work was used in southern Poland whenever a garment required a decorative hem or fringed hemstitching.

On men's clothing, drawn thread work was mainly limited to hemstitching, while on women's clothing hemstitching was combined with other needlework techniques. One of the items decorated just with hemstitch and a fringe was a kerchief used for wrapping a large prayer book while the book was carried to and from church. The same decoration was used on linen cloths covering the table on which a cross and a candle stood in the best room of a cottage in the Podhale region.

174

As women's clothing became more decorative, simple white shirts, once edged only with hemstitching, were embellished with rich ornamental details, such as eyelet and drawn thread designs arranged in alternating strips on the sleeves. The best, most sought-after embroideresses knew at least nine different varieties of drawn thread stitches. Until the end of the 19th century, all drawn thread work was done on linen with coarse white cotton thread.

In Spisz, in southern Poland, women embroidered elaborate blouses with drawn thread work on the sleeves and the front of the blouse and crocheted lace around the neckline.

Beautiful drawn thread work and stitching decorated kerchiefs, shawls, and aprons in southern and central Poland. Kerchiefs from Pszczyna combined crocheted lace on the outside edges, drawn thread work (with threads drawn from both the warp and weft of the fabric) on the inside edge, and eyelet embroidery in the center. Women in the villages south of Poznan embellished their white cotton aprons with drawn thread and colorful floral embroidery between the bands of horizontal pleats and bottom flounce. Sometimes a narrow ribbon was pulled in between the threads of the drawn thread strip to enrich the design.

In the mid-19th century, embroidered blouses, undergarments, aprons, and kerchiefs incorporated eyelet work, satin-stitch elements, and drawn thread work that filled large, irregular motifs with a net-like pattern (Fig. 7–1). Some of the more famous centers of that embroidery were Makow Podhalanski, Lancut, Szczawnica, and several villages around Krakow, Tarnow, and Rzeszow. The fashionable new designs were embroidered on the collars, sleeves, and fronts of women's blouses and on white linen skirts, aprons, kerchiefs, shawls, and bonnets. The designs were mainly floral, with motifs of roses, pansies, and sunflowers and sometimes small hearts. The centers of the flowers usually were filled with drawn thread work. The designs were almost always symmetrical, and often the same pattern was repeated on the collar, sleeves, and shirt front. Collars and aprons were edged with scallops, and each scallop contained a drawn thread element. White aprons from around Rzeszow were so wide and long that they often covered three-quarters of the skirt, and the beauty of the embroidery and the large areas of drawn thread work added a grand elegance to the costume. Richly embroidered petticoats were often made longer than the skirt in order to add one more decorative layer so that it could be seen at all times and not only during the vigorous spins and turns of dancing.

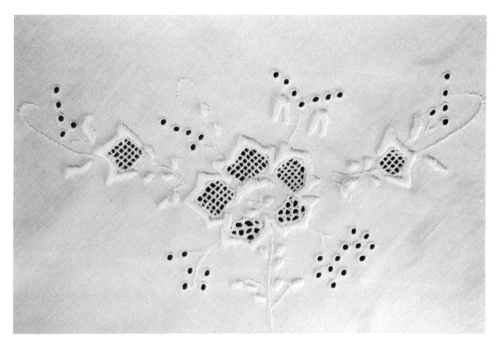

Fig. 7–1 A typical floral motif on a tablecloth from Makow Podhalanski.

The same combination of drawn thread work, eyelet embroidery, and satin-stitch elements can be seen in the long white shawls worn over the head for special occasions such as weddings, christenings, and Sunday Masses, as well as kerchiefs, which boasted elaborate designs placed in the corners. Cotton bonnets in Lower Silesia were embroidered in a similar fashion, although they were made from floral prints rather than white fabric. Ribbons were attached to the back of the bonnets and decorated with floral patterns.

Today, drawn thread work is used on household items more than on folk costumes.

DRAWN THREAD WORK TECHNIQUE

Drawn thread work can be used on table and bed linens, decorative items, and on garments such as blouses, skirts, nightshirts, aprons, and children's clothes, but it must be done on fabric with a distinctive weave, such as linen and heavy cottons, so that the threads of the weave can be

176

pulled with relative ease. Traditionally, hemstitching (the stitching that finishes the top and the bottom edges of the withdrawn section) was done in fine thread matching the fabric of the background, while the decorative stitching on the leftover threads was completed in heavier thread. Now free experimentation with a variety of threads allows more room for creativity. Embroidery hoops and frames can be used to control thread tension while working on larger pieces of drawn thread, but they are not necessary for smaller projects. Polish country embroideresses never used hoops or frames for drawn thread work.

The first step in drawn thread work is pulling out the threads from the background fabric. This process is simple if the design involves drawing thread only from the warp or weft of the fabric, where the thread can be withdrawn from one end to the other. First, a thread is pulled delicately with a pin until it is long enough to be held between the fingers. Then it is slowly withdrawn from the whole length of fabric. Next, several adjacent threads are pulled out.

The number of threads withdrawn depends on the width of the design. If drawn thread work is being used as a hem, the width of the hem has to be measured and marked with a pin before the threads are pulled out, and only at that distance from the edge can the first thread be withdrawn. Then the hem can be folded up to the line of the withdrawn thread and secured with running stitch. The work is turned to the wrong side and hemstitched along one or both edges. For hemstitching, usually four or five threads are withdrawn and each cluster is created from the three or four threads.

Withdrawing threads in two directions, from both warp and weft of the fabric, is more complicated because the corners of the piece must be perfectly square. The first step is to measure the hem allowance and mark the first thread to be withdrawn. The marking is done with pins in the middle of each side. Next, each of the four threads is cut in the middle and picked with a pin on all four sides interchangeably until each pair meets at the corner. Then each thread is cut about 1½" from the corner (Fig. 7–2). The rest of the threads can be withdrawn and cut in the same way. The loose ends can be turned to the wrong side and secured with a few stitches. Finally, the corners can be mitered and the hem turned up to the line of withdrawn thread and hemstitched, following the sequence in Figures 7–3, 7–4, and 7–5. Either a ladder or trellis hemstitch can be used (Fig. 7–6).

If the drawn thread design is elaborate, more threads have to be withdrawn to form a wider strip for the decorative stitches to be applied after

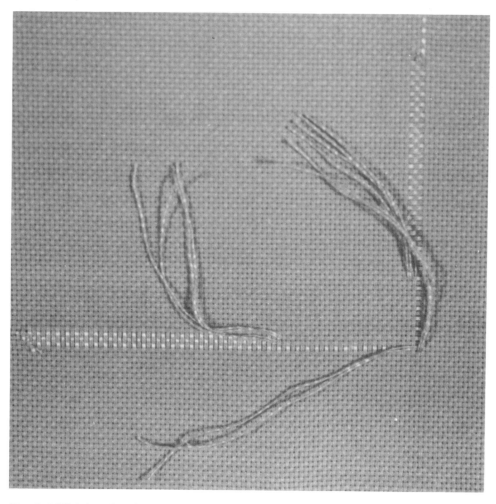

Fig. 7–2 Withdrawing threads in two directions, i.e., from both the warp and weft of the fabric.

completing the hemstitching, although the hemstitching can be omitted altogether. Any decorative stitches can be used, such as single crossing stitch, clusters with coral stitch, and lattice with herringbone stitch.

The corners can be finished with buttonhole stitch or filled with decorative stitching such as woven spiderwebs.

In the drawn thread floral patterns from Makow Podhalanski and the areas around Rzeszow and Krakow, the outline of the design is covered

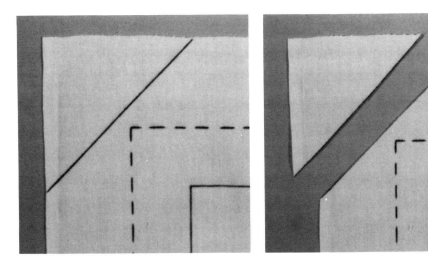

Fig. 7–3 Marking the corner to be mitered. Fig. 7–4 Trimming off excess fabric.

with running stitch and then with buttonhole stitch worked over the running stitch. The threads are cut close to the buttonholed edge and withdrawn in both directions from the inside of the motif. The threads are withdrawn in intervals, withdrawing two threads and leaving two in place. The remaining grid of the threads is strengthened with an overcast

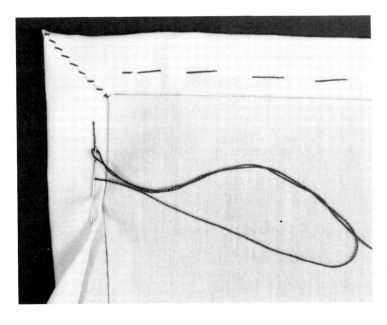

Fig. 7–5 Turning the fabric and stitching to finish the corner neatly.

179

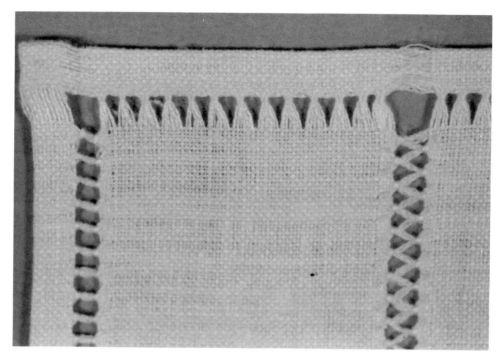

Fig. 7–6 Single hemstitch (shown along top) is done on just one side of the withdrawn thread, with ladder hemstitch (on the left) and trellis hemstitch (on the right).

stitch. However, in Polish peasant embroideries from other areas, cutting and withdrawing the threads is done *after* covering the outline of each motif with running stitch. The grid is overcast and the edges strengthened also with overcast stitch, which hides the raw edge and the running stitch (Fig. 7–7). Embroidery in satin stitch is added to complete the design.

This whole process can be reversed and, instead of a grid motif, the background itself could be gridded so that the work resembles *Russian drawn ground work*. Here the buttonhole stitch has to be reversed so that the looped edge faces the gridded background rather than the inside of the motif.

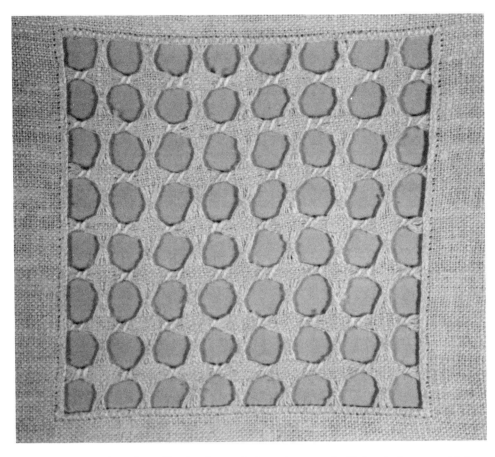

Fig. 7–7 Drawn thread motif using buttonhole and overcast stitches to form a grid design.

181

Peasant Blouse

(Color plate 9, Figs. 7–8 and 7–9)

Materials

Pattern for a short-sleeve peasant-style blouse
White cotton fabric and sewing supplies for the blouse
Embroidery:
    White cotton embroidery floss
    White sewing thread
    Embroidery hoop
    Stiletto
    Needles
    Transfer tools

Instructions

The pattern in Figure 7–10 represents one-half of the design for the front of the blouse. Complete the drawing of the entire design and transfer it to the front of the blouse. Transfer the sleeve design (Fig. 7–11) to both sleeves.

With white sewing thread, outline with running stitch all the round eyelets and all the large shapes marked with a grid. Punch out the round eyelets with a stiletto and overcast with three strands of embroidery floss. Next, closely overcast all the grid-filled shapes, but do not cut out any fabric.

After overcasting the outlines, form the grid by withdrawing several threads from the background fabric in regular intervals and in both directions. Cut the threads to be withdrawn close to the overcast edge. Next, overcast the remaining grid in three strands of floss. (The number of withdrawn threads depends on the weave of the fabric.)

Complete the rest of the design in four strands of floss. All the stems are embroidered with stem stitch and all the leaves in satin stitch.

After finishing the embroidery, assemble the blouse and wash and iron it.

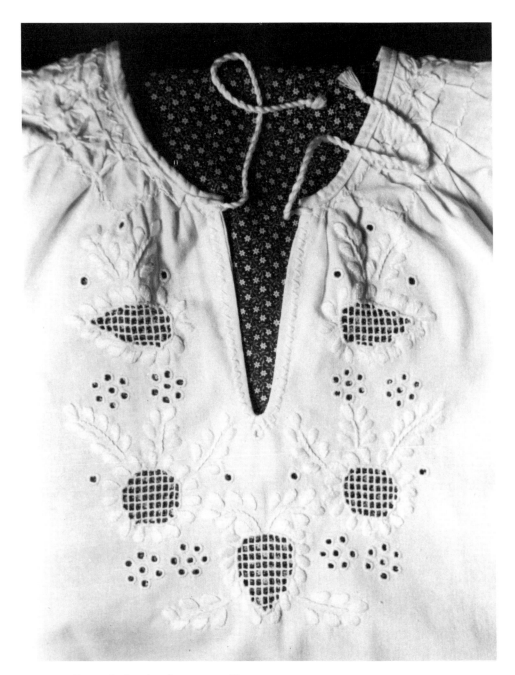

Fig. 7–8 Front design for the peasant blouse.

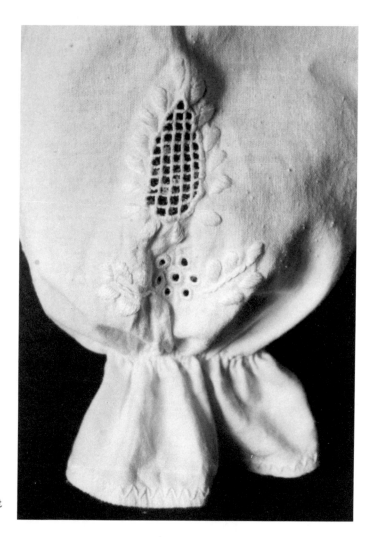

Fig. 7–9 The sleeve
design on the peasant
blouse.

Pattern explanations

Solid motifs represent eyelets.
Grids represent drawn thread motifs.
Outlined motifs are embroidered with satin stitch.
Curving lines are embroidered with stem stitch.

184

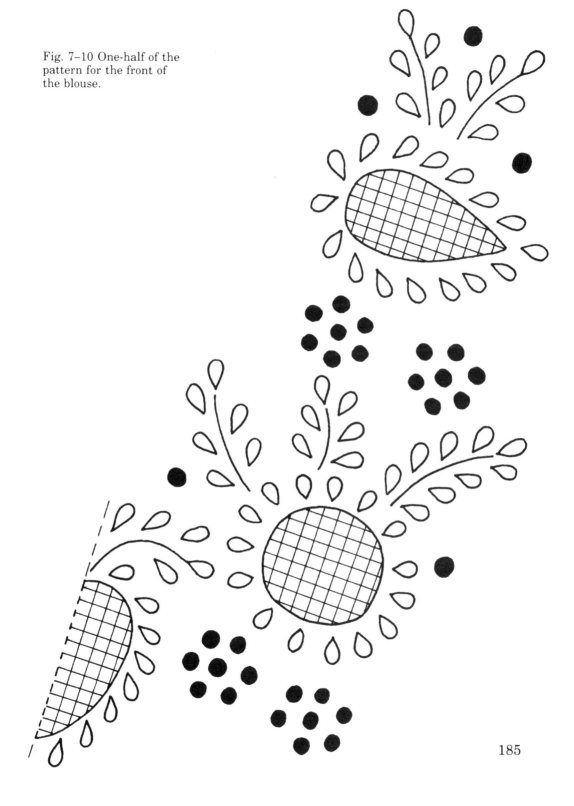

Fig. 7–10 One-half of the pattern for the front of the blouse.

185

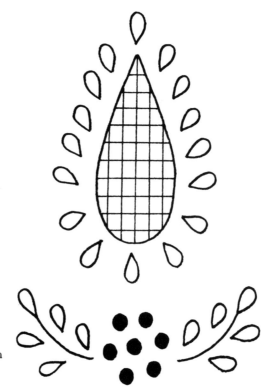

Fig. 7–11 Pattern
for the blouse
sleeve.

Sachet

(Color plate 15 and Fig. 7–12)

Finished size: 5¼″ by 6¼″

Materials

Two 6¼″ by 7¼″ rectangles of white Hardanger cloth
White embroidery floss (two skeins)
White sewing thread
Needles
Embroidery hoop
Stiletto
20″ of light-pink satin ribbon (¼″ wide)
Transfer tools

Instructions

Note: The pattern does not include seam allowances. Remember to add
seam allowances before cutting out the pattern.

Following pattern in Figure 7–13, mark on one piece of fabric where
the threads will be withdrawn and withdraw enough threads to equal the
width of strips ("a" and "b"). On the second piece of cloth, mark and withdraw just the top strip of thread ("b").

Next, hem the top of both pieces so that the edge of the folded hem
lines up with the top edge of the withdrawn-thread strip. Hemstitch all the
withdrawn-thread strips forming ladder hemstitch. Stitching is done in
two strands of embroidery floss.

Transfer the floral pattern onto the fabric (Fig. 7–14), lining up the
bottom edge of the needlework design with the broken line in the pattern.
With white sewing thread, outline in running stitch all the round eyelets
and the central tear-shaped motif. Punch out the round eyelets with a stiletto and overcast the edges. Now, closely overcast the tear-shaped motif.

After overcasting, cut and withdraw threads in both directions and in
regular intervals (withdrawing two, then leaving two) from the inside of
the motif. Overcast the remaining grid. Complete the design by embroidering the leaves in satin stitch and the leaf stems in stem stitch.

Assemble the bag and pull the ribbon into the top strip of ladder
stitch.

187

Fig. 7–12 Sachet.

Pattern explanations

Double lines around the tear-shaped motif are embroidered in overcast stitch.

The grid shows the area of withdrawn thread.

Solid circles represent eyelets.

Outlined leaves are filled with satin stitch.

Stems are embroidered in stem stitch.

188

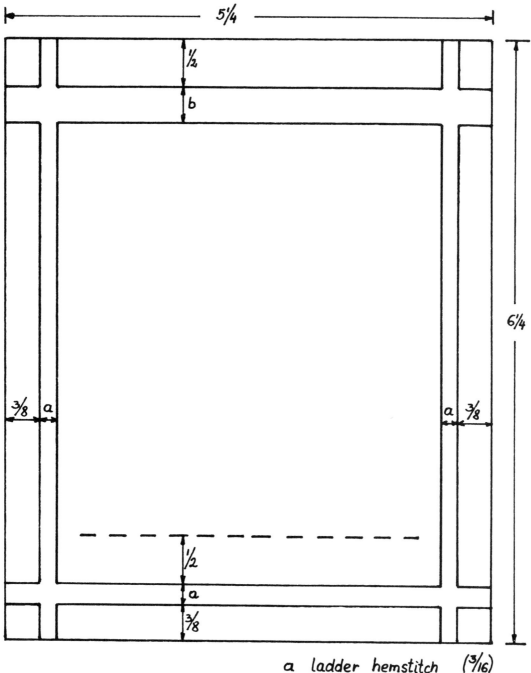

Fig. 7–13 Pattern for the sachet.

a *ladder hemstitch* $(3/16)$
b *ladder hemstitch* $(3/8)$

Fig. 7–14 Motif for the sachet.

Apron
(Color plate 13, Figs. 7–15 and 7–16)

Finished size: 28″ from the waist

Materials

30″ by 36½″ rectangle of cream-colored linen
12″ by 14″ rectangle of cream-colored linen for the bib
Strips of linen for the waistband and neck strap
Blue pearl cotton No. 8 (one ball)
White sewing thread
Needles

Instructions

Note: The patterns do not include seam allowances.

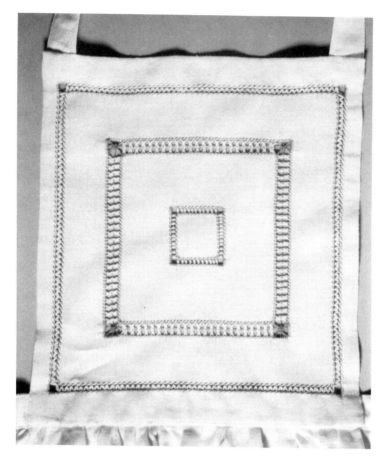

Fig. 7–15 Apron bib.

Following the pattern in Figure 7–17, withdraw a ¼″-wide strip of thread along the two shorter edges and one longer edge of the skirt. Remembering to add seam allowance, place the strip ½″ from the edges of the finished apron.

Next, withdraw the other two strips of thread, marked "b" and "c" on the pattern. Hem the three sides of the skirt and miter the two bottom corners.

Embroider the strips of withdrawn thread with decorative stitching. Strip "a" is embroidered in ladder hemstitch, strip "b" in lattice with herringbone stitch, and strip "c" in double crossing stitch. All stitching is done in one strand of pearl cotton.

191

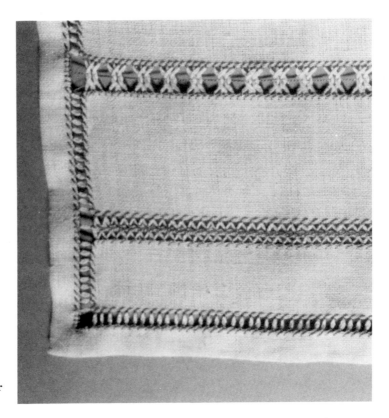

Fig. 7–16 A corner
of the apron skirt.

After completing the skirt, embroider the bib. The pattern in Figure
7–18 gives the widths of the withdrawn thread strips and the names of the
stitches. (Remember to add seam allowances.)

After completing all the stitching, assemble the apron by gathering
the skirt and sewing on the waistband, bib, and neck strap. Wash and iron
the apron.

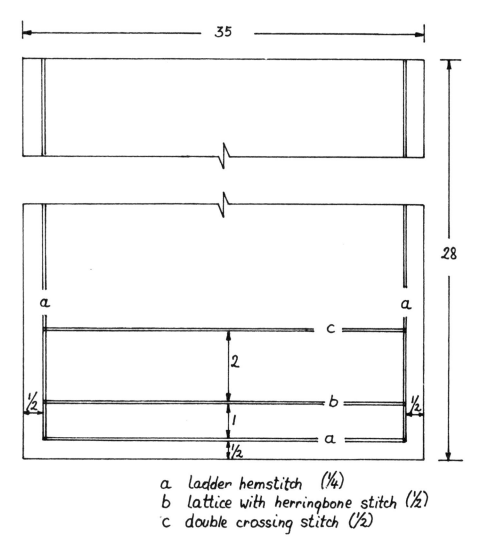

a ladder hemstitch (¼)
b lattice with herringbone stitch (½)
c double crossing stitch (½)

Fig. 7–17 Pattern for the apron skirt.

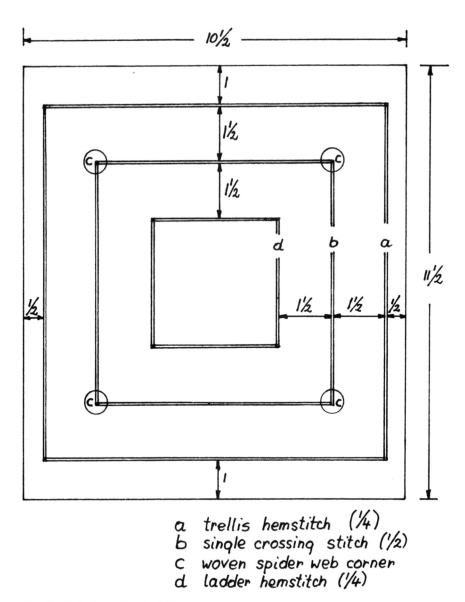

a trellis hemstitch (¼)
b single crossing stitch (½)
c woven spider web corner
d ladder hemstitch (¼)

Fig. 7–18 Pattern for the bib.

194

Table Runner
(Color plate 14, Fig. 7–19)

Finished size: 29″ by 51″

Materials
36½″ by 59″ rectangle of cream-colored linen
White pearl cotton No. 5
White sewing thread
Needles

Instructions
Note: The patterns do not include seam allowances. Allow 3¾″ on each of the long edges and 4″ on each of the short edges.

Following the patterns in Figure 7–20 and 7–21, withdraw threads in regular intervals from one edge to the other. Each withdrawn strip and the distance between each pair of strips is ½″. Along each edge of the cloth, withdraw six strips. Instead of decorating the edges of the strips with hemstitching, pull one strand of pearl cotton through the middle of each strip to create a single crossing stitch. Where the pearl-cotton strands cross under a 90° angle, twist one strand over the other to secure. (*Note:* Each strand of pearl cotton has to be long enough to complete the whole journey from one end of the fabric to the other.)

Hem the table runner on the wrong side.

This is a fast project that skips some of the stages in drawn thread work and so the finished product is less sturdy. Wash and iron the piece carefully and gently.

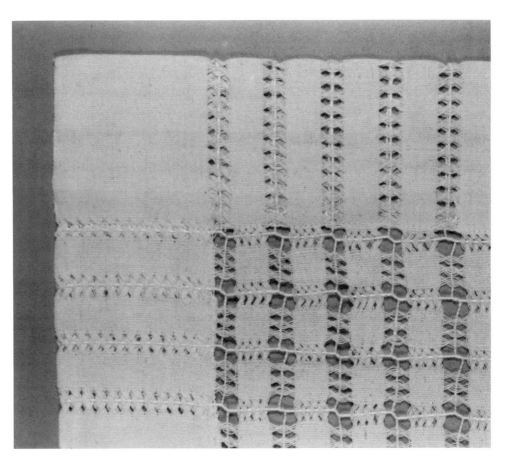

Fig. 7–19 One corner of the table runner.

196

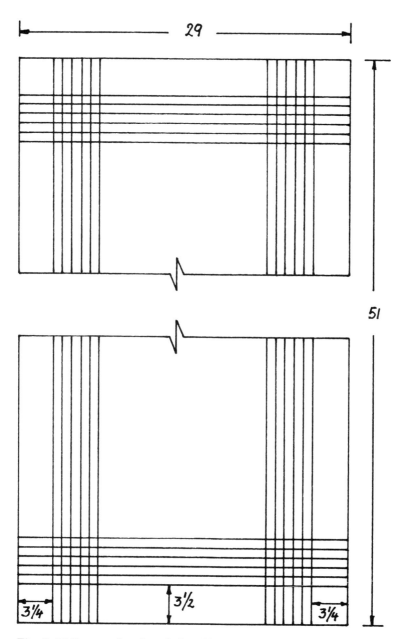

Fig. 7–20 Pattern for the whole table runner.

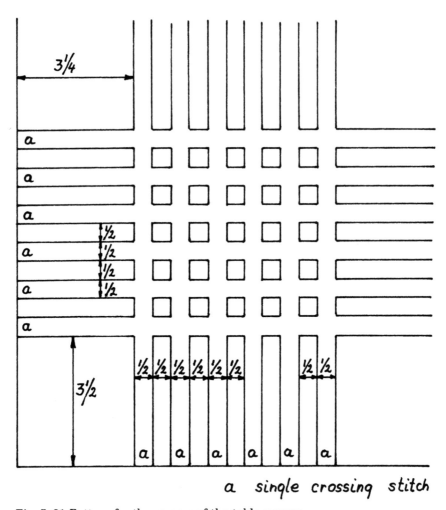

Fig. 7–21 Pattern for the corners of the table runner.

Pot Holders
(Color plate 12, Figs. 7–22 and 7–23)

Finished size: 9" by 9"

Materials for a redbird pot holder

8" by 8" square of beige 14-count aida cloth
Blue pearl cotton No. 8 (one ball)
Red embroidery floss (one skein)
Two 10" by 10" squares of red floral print
Red sewing thread
Needles
Embroidery hoop
Small amount of fiberfill

Materials for a bluebird pot holder

8" by 8" square of cream-colored 14–count aida cloth
Red pearl cotton No. 8 (one ball)
Blue embroidery floss (one skein)
Two 10" by 10" squares of red floral print
Red sewing thread
Needles
Embroidery hoop
Small amount of fiberfill

Instructions

Note: The patterns in Figures 7–24 and 7–26 do not include seam allowances.

Decorate each square according to the patterns. The patterns indicate the width of the drawn thread strips and the names of the stitches. All stitching is done in one strand of pearl cotton. The cross-stitch motifs are embroidered in three strands of embroidery floss. On the redbird pot holder (Fig. 7–25), the birds are stitched in red and the drawn thread work in blue. On the bluebird pot holder (Fig. 7–27), the colors are reversed.

Fig. 7–22 Redbird pot holder.

After completing the stitching, center the hemmed aida cloth square on the right side of one of the floral print squares and stitch together, using one of the decorative stitches and one strand of pearl cotton. (I used a combination of running stitch and cross stitch.)

Assemble each pot holder and pad it lightly with fiberfill. Attach a loop made out of ribbon or a scrap of fabric to one corner of the pot holder.

Fig. 7–23 Bluebird pot holder.

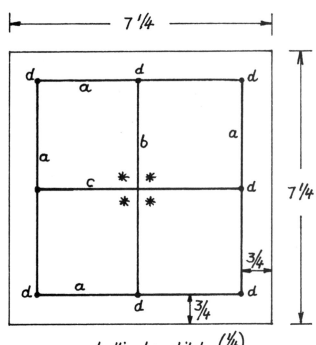

a   trellis hemstitch $(1/4)$
b   ladder hemstitch $(3/16)$
c   single crossing stitch $(3/16)$
d   woven spider web corner
*   cross stitch birds

Fig. 7–24 Pattern for the redbird pot holder.

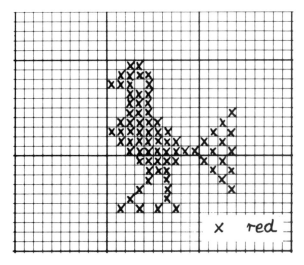

x   red

Fig. 7–25 Cross stitch chart for the redbird pot holder.

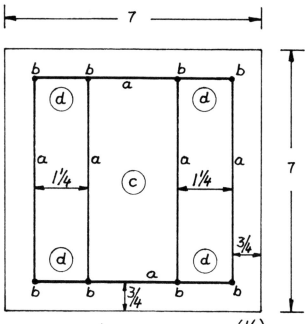

a single crossing stitch (¼)
b woven spider web corner
c cross stitch flower
d cross stitch bird

Fig. 7–26 Pattern for the bluebird pot holder.

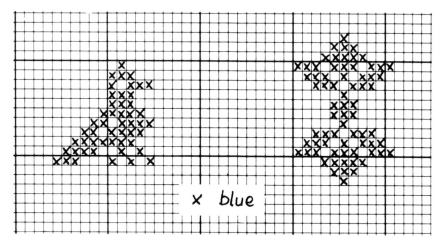

x blue

Fig. 7–27 Cross stitch chart for the bluebird pot holder.

Square Pillow
(Color plate 16, Fig. 7–28)

Finished size: 13½″ by 13½″, plus cord trim

Materials

14½″ by 14½″ square of natural unbleached linen
Two 14½″ by 14½″ squares of unbleached muslin
White sewing thread
Approximately 60″ of beige cord
Needles
Fiberfill

Instructions

Note: The pattern does not indicate seam allowances.

Following the pattern in Figure 7–29, mark the point where the threads will be withdrawn for the first strip. It is easiest to start with the four strips that form a frame along the edges of the pillow ½″ from each edge. Remember to add seam allowances. Withdraw the rest of the strips. Each of the withdrawn thread strips is ¼″ wide and decorated with ladder hemstitch in one strand of white sewing thread. After completing the stitching, wash and iron the piece.

Assemble the pillow, stuff with fiberfill, and sew the cord to the edges.

Fig. 7–28 Square pillow.

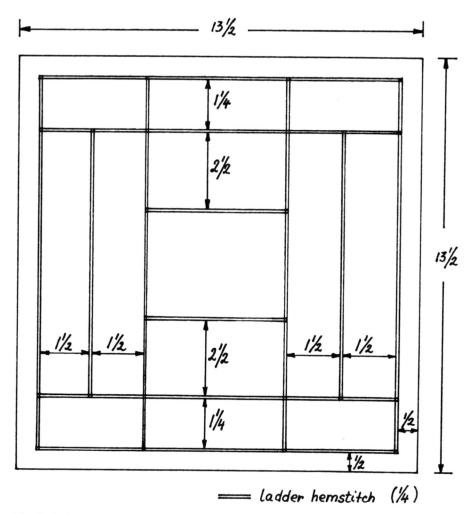

Fig. 7–29 Pattern for the square pillow.

Sampler Pillow
(Color plate 16, Fig. 7–30)

Finished size: 12½" by 17", plus cord trim

Materials
13½" by 18" rectangle of natural unbleached linen
Two 13½" by 18" rectangles of unbleached muslin
Brown pearl cotton No. 8 (one ball)
Approximately 63" of brown decorative cord
Sewing thread
Needles
Fiberfill

Instructions
Note: The pattern does not include seam allowances.

Following the pattern in Figure 7–31, mark the points where the threads will be withdrawn for the first strip ("a"). Remembering to add seam allowances, place it 1½" from one of the shorter edges of the pillow and ½" from the longer edges. The strip will be ½" wide and decorated with single crossing stitch. Then, 1½" from strip "a", withdraw threads for strip "b", which will be ⅝" wide and decorated with lattice single crossing stitch. Follow the pattern for completing the rest of the strips. They are of varying widths, but the distance between each pair of strips is always 1½". The short edges of each strip are secured with buttonhole stitch. All stitching is done in one strand of pearl cotton.

After completing the sampler, wash and iron it. Then assemble the pillow, stuff it with fiberfill, and sew the cord to the edges.

Fig. 7–30 Sampler pillow.

208

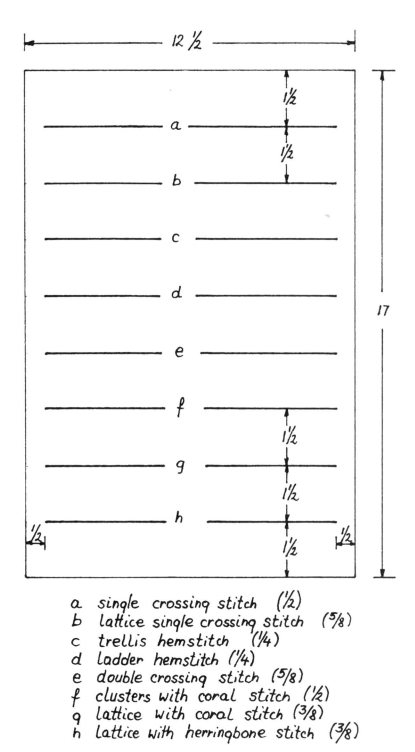

a single crossing stitch (½)
b lattice single crossing stitch (⅝)
c trellis hemstitch (¼)
d ladder hemstitch (¼)
e double crossing stitch (⅝)
f clusters with coral stitch (½)
g lattice with coral stitch (⅜)
h lattice with herringbone stitch (⅜)

Fig. 7–31 Pattern for the sampler pillow.

Rectangular Pillow
(Color plate 16, Fig. 7–32)

Finished size: 12½" by 15¼", plus cord trim

Materials
13½" by 16¼" rectangle of natural unbleached linen
Two 13½" by 16¼" rectangles of unbleached muslin
Yellow pearl cotton No. 8 (one ball)
Approximately 60" of yellow decorative cord
Sewing thread
Needles
Fiberfill

Instructions
Note: The pattern does not include seam allowances.

Following the pattern in Figure 7–33, mark the points where the threads will be withdrawn for the first strip ("a"). Remembering to add seam allowances, place it 1¼" from the edges of the finished pillow. This strip, which forms a frame around the whole pillow, is ¼" wide and decorated with ladder hemstitch in one strand of yellow pearl cotton.

Place the second, smaller frame ("b") 1¼" from the first one. The frame is ⅛" wide and decorated with overcast bars in one strand of pearl cotton. The third frame ("c"), placed 1¼" from the second one, is ⅛" wide and stitched with trellis hemstitch in one strand of pearl cotton. The smallest, innermost frame ("b") is also ⅛" wide and is decorated with overcast bars in one strand of pearl cotton. All raw edges in the corners formed by withdrawing thread are finished with buttonhole stitch.

After completing the stitching, wash and iron the piece. Assemble the pillow, stuff it with fiberfill, and sew the cord to the edges.

Fig. 7–32 Rectangular pillow.

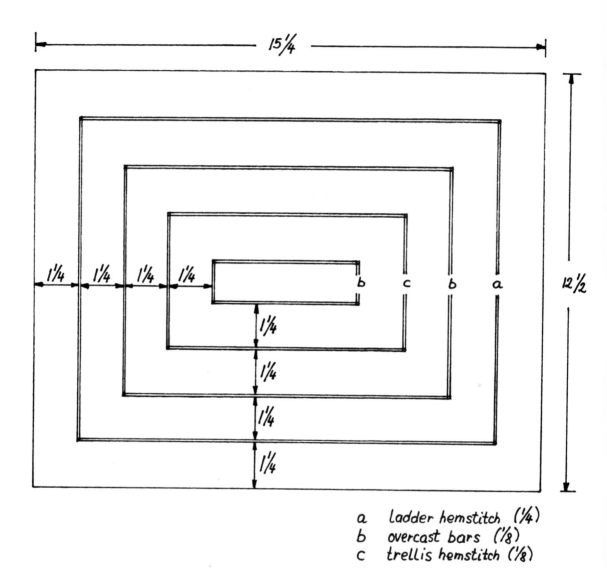

a   *ladder hemstitch* (¼)
b   *overcast bars* (⅛)
c   *trellis hemstitch* (⅛)

Fig. 7–33 Pattern for the rectangular pillow.

Kurpie Embroidery

ORIGINS OF A UNIQUE EMBROIDERY

North of Warsaw, in the region known as "White Forest Kurpie," a unique form of embroidery found its birthplace. Although it is based on standard embroidery stitches, the designs have no counterpart among other Polish types of stitchery. Kurpie designs are embroidered primarily in red with black accents and are always done by hand.

The designs are embroidered on women's shirts, also sewn by hand, which are usually knee-length and made from three different fabrics. The front, back, and sleeves are cut out of high-quality linen, and the collars, cuffs, and embroidered shoulder pieces are made out of cotton. The bottom of the shirt is coarse linen or a linen and cotton blend. Everyday shirts are simply decorated, while holiday shirts have collar and cuffs embroidered in red, or the collar stitched in white and the cuffs in red. Wedding shirts are embroidered entirely in white. The collar and cuffs are made out of a double piece of cloth and quilted with rows of running stitch in coarse thread; they are also edged with crocheted lace trims.

Kurpie designs employ overcast, chain, satin, stem, and feather stitches as well as the unique Kurpie stitch. The stitches form circles, half-circles, spirals, overcast holes, zigzags, triangles, squares, and stylized blossoms and plants. The collars, about 2½" wide, are decorated with four triple circles in each corner. The cuffs are embroidered with circles and plants, while the shoulders are decorated with half-circles, blossoms, and geometrical figures. The whole composition is underlined and framed with a variety of stitches and each element delicately outlined in black stitching.

Kurpie embroidery was originally done in linen thread and later in cotton flosses, which were purchased in town on market days. The linen

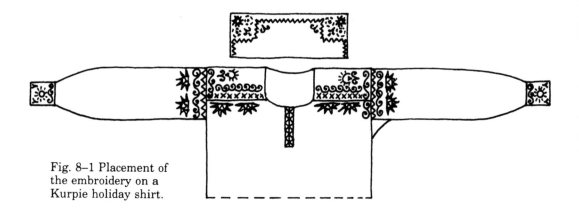

Fig. 8–1 Placement of
the embroidery on a
Kurpie holiday shirt.

and cotton cloth for the shirts were usually made at home. Shortly before
the Second World War, Kurpie women also began to decorate table linens
and kerchiefs and sold them in nearby cities and towns.

North of "White Forest Kurpie," in the region of "Green Forest
Kurpie," the embroidery was much simpler, although it evolved from a
common ancestry. Here the shirts were made out of thin white cloth and
embroidered in white (with a rare addition of red or blue) in backstitch,

Fig. 8–2 Kurpie cir-
cle motif.

214

Fig. 8–3 Kurpie plant motif.

running stitch, and chain stitch. The Kurpie women also decorated towels and aprons with designs adapted from favorite paper-cutout patterns. Some of the cutouts were similar to the popular circle motifs used in the needlework designs from "White Forest Kurpie." Not only the shapes used in the two art forms bear resemblance, but also the overall color scheme. The colors of Kurpie embroideries and paper cutouts are subdued with one- or two-color arrangements; while, for example, the extremely bright costumes and needlework from Lowicz find their counterparts in multicolored cutouts from the same region. And so the relationship between the different art forms in a region is witness to the tastes, tradition and aesthetic sensitivity of its people.

Fig. 8–4 Half-circle Kurpie motif.

215

Round Kurpie Doily
(Fig. 8–5)

Finished size: 6¼" in diameter

Materials

8" by 8" square of natural unbleached linen
Red embroidery floss
Black embroidery floss
Sewing thread to match the linen
Needles
Transfer tools
Optional:
    White crochet cotton
    Crochet hook

Instructions

Note: Figure 8–6 shows the full-size doily but does not include seam allowances.

Transfer the pattern onto the fabric. The embroidery is completed in satin stitch, running stitch, chain stitch, and Kurpie stitch. The embroidery is predominantly red with accents in black. All stitching is done in two strands of floss.

After completing the embroidery, trim the excess fabric and hem the piece carefully to form an even circle. A very narrow edging can be also crocheted with white crochet cotton.

Wash and iron the doily.

Pattern explanations

All solid areas are embroidered in satin stitch.
Looped lines are embroidered in chain stitch.
Broken lines are embroidered in running stitch.
Zigzags and "V" shapes are embroidered in Kurpie stitch.

Fig. 8–5 Round Kurpie doily.

Fig. 8–6 Pattern for the round doily.

218

Square Tablecloth from Kurpie
(See cover photo and Fig. 8–7)

Finished size: 40″ by 40″

Materials
41½″ by 41½″ square of natural unbleached linen
Red embroidery floss
Black embroidery floss
Sewing thread to match the linen
Needles
Transfer tools

Instructions
Note: The pattern in Figure 8–8 shows the finished size of the tablecloth
and does not include hem allowances.

First, hem the piece of linen so that it measures 40″ by 40″. Next, embroider all four edges of the square with a row of Kurpie stitch in red floss,
taking two strands at a time. Make the stitch about ¼″ wide (marked "a"
on the pattern). After completing the edging, measure 8″ from each edge
and mark an inner "frame" 1″ wide (marked "b" on the pattern). Fill the
frame with five rows of Kurpie stitch. The middle row is embroidered in
black and the outer rows are stitched in red. Stitching is done in two
strands of floss.

The pattern in Figure 8–9 represents one-half of the design. Complete
the pattern and transfer it into each corner of the square created by the inner frame. Now, embroider each corner. All the stitching is done in two
strands of embroidery floss. The embroidery is predominantly red with
black accents.

Wash and iron the tablecloth.

Pattern explanations
All solid areas are embroidered in satin stitch.
Looped lines are embroidered in chain stitch.
Broken lines are embroidered in running stitch.
Zigzags and "V" shapes are embroidered in Kurpie stitch.

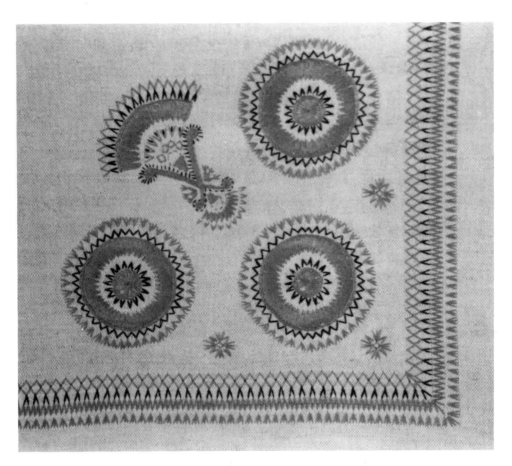

Fig. 8–7 Corner design for the tablecloth.

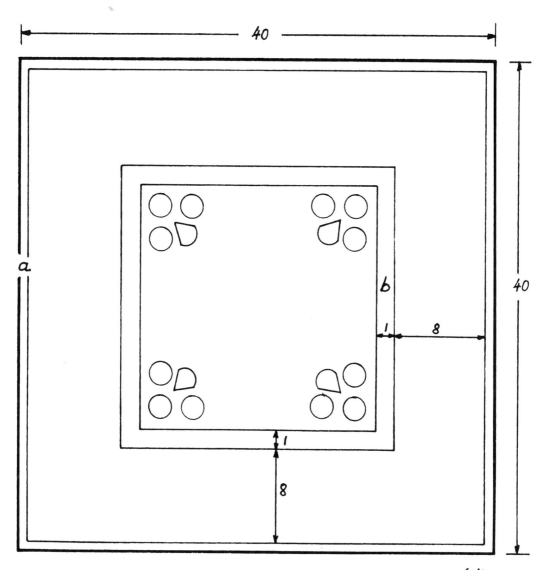

a one row of Kurpie stitch in red (¼)
b five rows of Kurpie stitch ; the middle
   one in black; the other four in
   red

Fig. 8–8 Pattern for the square tablecloth.

221

Fig. 8–9 One-half of the embroidery pattern
for a corner of the tablecloth.

Kurpie Placemat

(Color plate 18)

Finished size: 12″ by 20″

Materials

14″ by 22″ rectangle of cream-colored linen
Red embroidery floss
Black embroidery floss
White sewing thread
Needles
Transfer tools

Instructions

Note: The pattern in Figure 8–10 does not include seam allowances.

First, hem the piece of linen so that it measures 12″ by 20″. Next, embroider the edges with three rows of Kurpie stitch for a width of ½″. The middle row is embroidered in black and the outer rows are stitched in red. Stitching is done in two strands of floss.

Transfer the embroidery pattern (Fig. 8–11) into each one of the four corners of the placemat (see the pattern). Now, embroider each corner. All the embroidery is done in two strands of floss and red is the predominant color.

Wash and iron the placemat.

Pattern explanations

Solid areas are embroidered in satin stitch.
Looped lines are embroidered in chain stitch.
Broken lines are embroidered in running stitch.
Zigzags and "V" shapes are embroidered in Kurpie stitch.

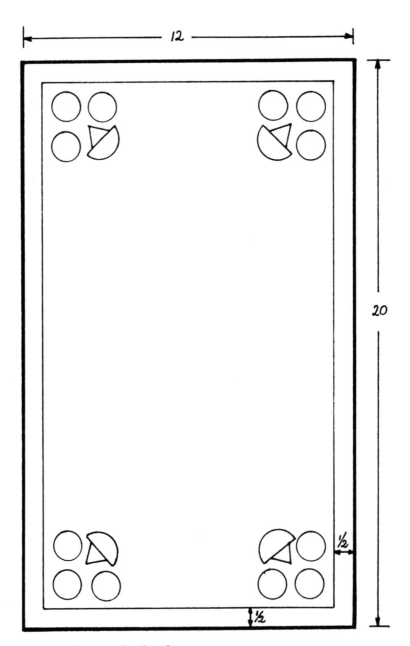

Fig. 8–10 Pattern for the placemat.

Fig. 8–11 Embroidery pattern for one corner of the placemat.

Selected Bibliography

Atlas Polskich Strojow Ludowych. Seria. Polskie Towarzystwo Ludowoznawcze w Poznaniu.

Boyle, Elizabeth. *The Irish Flowerers.* Ulster Folk Museum and Institute of Irish Studies, Queen's University, Belfast, 1971.

Carter, Michael. *Crafts in China.* New York: Doubleday, 1977.

Cavallo, Adolph S. *Needlework.* The Smithsonian Illustrated Library of Antiques. New York: Cooper-Hewitt Museum.

Cave, Oenone. *Cut-work Embroidery and How to do It.* New York: Dover Publications, 1982.

Chmielinska, Aniela. *Ksiezacy i Ich Stroj.* Warsaw: Wydawnictwo Polskiej Macierzy Szkolnej, 1930.

Cichowicz, Wieslawa. "Haft Wielkopolski i Czepce Wielkopolskie." *Polska Sztuka Ludowa,* No. 7–8 (1949).

Czarnecka, Irena. *Polska Sztuka Ludowa.* Warsaw: Polonia, 1958.

Dean, Beryl. *Ecclesiastical Embroidery.* Boston: Charles T. Branford Company.

Digby, George Wingfield. *Elizabethan Embroidery.* London: Faber and Faber, 1963.

Feldman, Annette. *Handmade Lace and Patterns.* New York: Harper and Row, 1975.

Frankowski, Eugeniusz. "Hafty Kurpiowskie." *Polska Sztuka Ludowa,* No. 6 (1953).

Glapa, Adam. "Wielkopolski Haft Snutkowy." *Polska Sztuka Ludowa,* No. 4 (1955).

Grodecka, Zofia. "Babimojsko-Dabrowiecki Haft Przewlekany." *Polska Sztuka Ludowa,* No. 2 (1967).

Hofsinde, Robert. *Indian Beadwork.* New York: William Morrow, 1958.

Hughes, Therle. *English Domestic Needlework 1660–1860*. New York: Macmillan, 1961.

Huish, Marcus B. *Samplers and Tapestry Embroidery*. New York: Dover Publications, 1970.

Jones, Mary Eirwen. *The Romance of Lace*. London: Springbooks.

Jourdain, M. *The History of English Secular Embroidery*. London: Kegan Paul, Trench, Trubner and Co., 1910.

Kendrick, A. F. *English Needlework*. London: A. & C. Black, 1933.

Kozaczka, Grażyna. *Polish Embroidery Workbook with Patterns*. Cazenovia, N.Y. 1982.

Kozaczka, Grażyna. *Polish Needlework Patterns — Cutwork, Goldwork, Beadwork*. Cazenovia, N.Y. 1985.

Lewicka, Anna Kowalska. "Haft Bialy na Podhalu." *Polska Sztuka Ludowa*, No. 4 (1957).

Mankowski, Tadeusz. *Polskie Tkaniny i Hafty XVI–XVIII Wieku*. Wroclaw: Zaklad im. Ossolinskich, 1954.

Modzelewska, Wanda. "Pare Uwag o Przewlekaniu Na Tiulu." *Polska Sztuka Ludowa*, No. 2 (1949).

Nylen, Anna-Maja. *Swedish Handcraft*. New York: Van Nostrand Reinhold, 1977.

Preston, Doris Campbell. *Needle-Made Laces and Net Embroideries*. New York: Dover Publications, 1984.

Reinfuss, R., and J. Swiderski. *Sztuka Ludowa w Polsce*. Krakow, 1960.

Schuette, Marie, and Sigrid Muller-Christensen. *A Pictoral History of Embroidery*. New York: Frederic A. Praeger, 1964.

Snook, Barbara. *English Historical Embroidery*. London: B. T. Batsford, 1960.

Swain, M. H. *The Flowerers*. Edinburgh: W. & R. Chambers, 1955.

Swan, Susan Burrows. *A Winterthur Guide to American Needlework*. A Winterthur Book/Rutledge Books. New York: Crown Publishers, 1976.

Swift, Gay. *The Larousse Encyclopedia of Embroidery Techniques*. New York: Larousse, 1984.

Thomas, Mary. *Mary Thomas's Embroidery Book*. New York: Dover Publications, 1983.

Udziela, Seweryn. *Ludowe Stroje Krakowskie i ich Kroj*. Nakladem Muzeum Etnograficznego w Krakowie, 1930.

White, Mary. *How to Do Beadwork*. New York: Doubleday, 1904.

Index

Page numbers in *italic* indicate information in illustrations.

228